THE
MIRACLE SEED

MARTIN LEMELMAN has illustrated over thirty children's books and is the author-illustrator of the graphic memoirs *Two Cents Plain* (Bloomsbury) and *Mendel's Daughter* (Free Press). He hopes that *The Miracle Seed* inspires his granddaughters and other young women to ask hard questions about the world and persevere in the fields of science, technology, engineering, and math. Martin lives in Florida, where he is a certified Florida Master Gardener. Visit Martin's website at twocentcomics.com and follow him on Twitter @MartinLemelman.

Text and illustrations © 2023 Martin Lemelman

Published in 2023 by
Eerdmans Books for Young Readers
an imprint of Wm. B. Eerdmans Publishing Co.
Grand Rapids, Michigan

www.eerdmans.com/youngreaders

Manufactured in Canada

31 30 29 28 27 26 25 24 23   1 2 3 4 5 6 7 8 9

ISBN 978-0-8028-5590-9

A catalog record of this book is available from the Library of Congress.

Illustrations created digitally

This book is about historical events, but the dialogue included
has been imagined for the purposes of storytelling.

THE
MIRACLE SEED

MARTIN LEMELMAN

EERDMANS BOOKS FOR YOUNG READERS

GRAND RAPIDS, MICHIGAN

To Dr. Elaine Solowey,
who patiently answered all my questions.
I hope I've done justice to your miracle.

To my amazing grandchildren,
Jason, William, Andrew, Oliver, Jeffrey,
Hannah, Abigail, Zoja, and Jack—
all miracles.

— M. L.

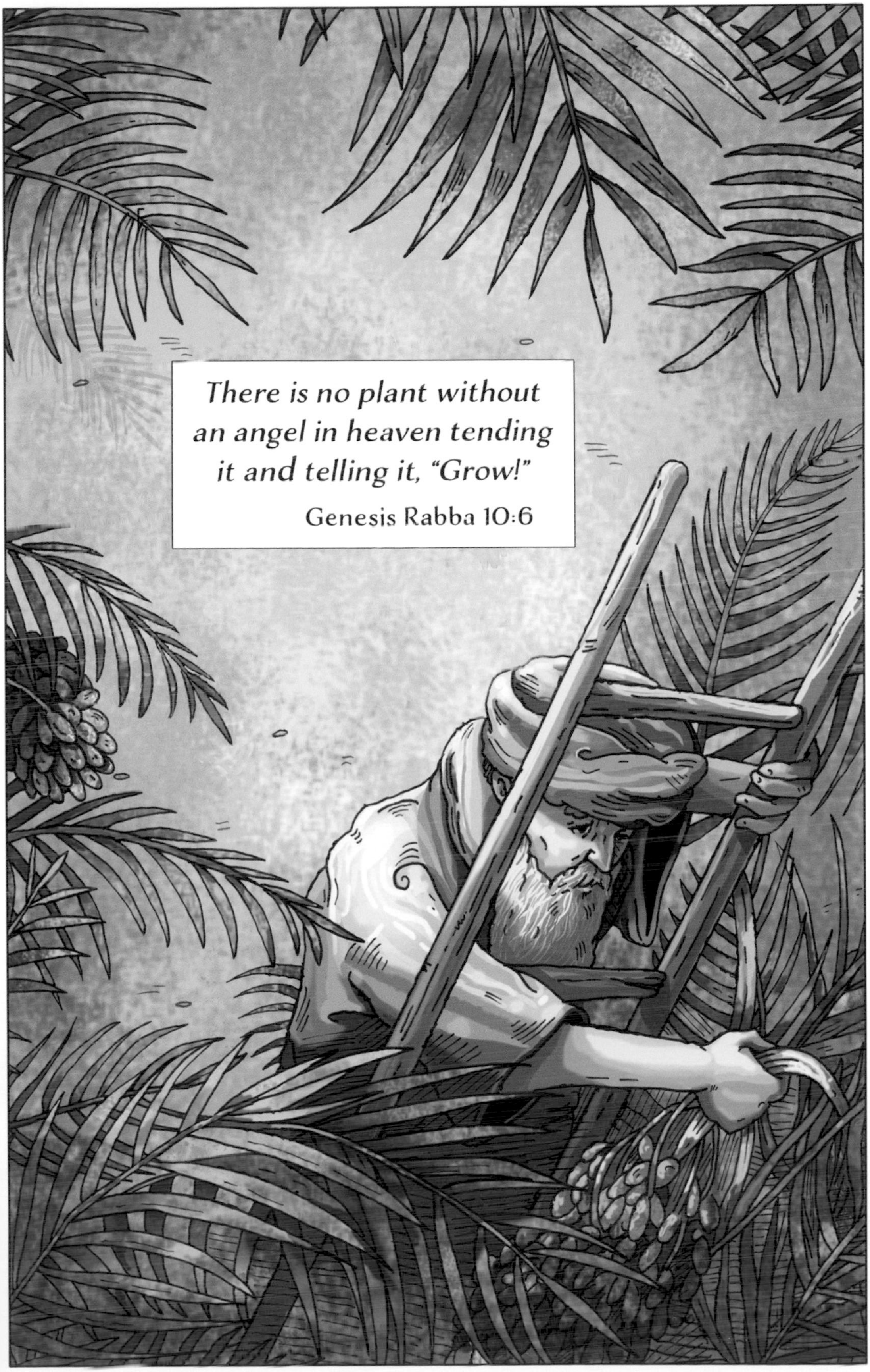
There is no plant without an angel in heaven tending it and telling it, "Grow!"
Genesis Rabba 10:6

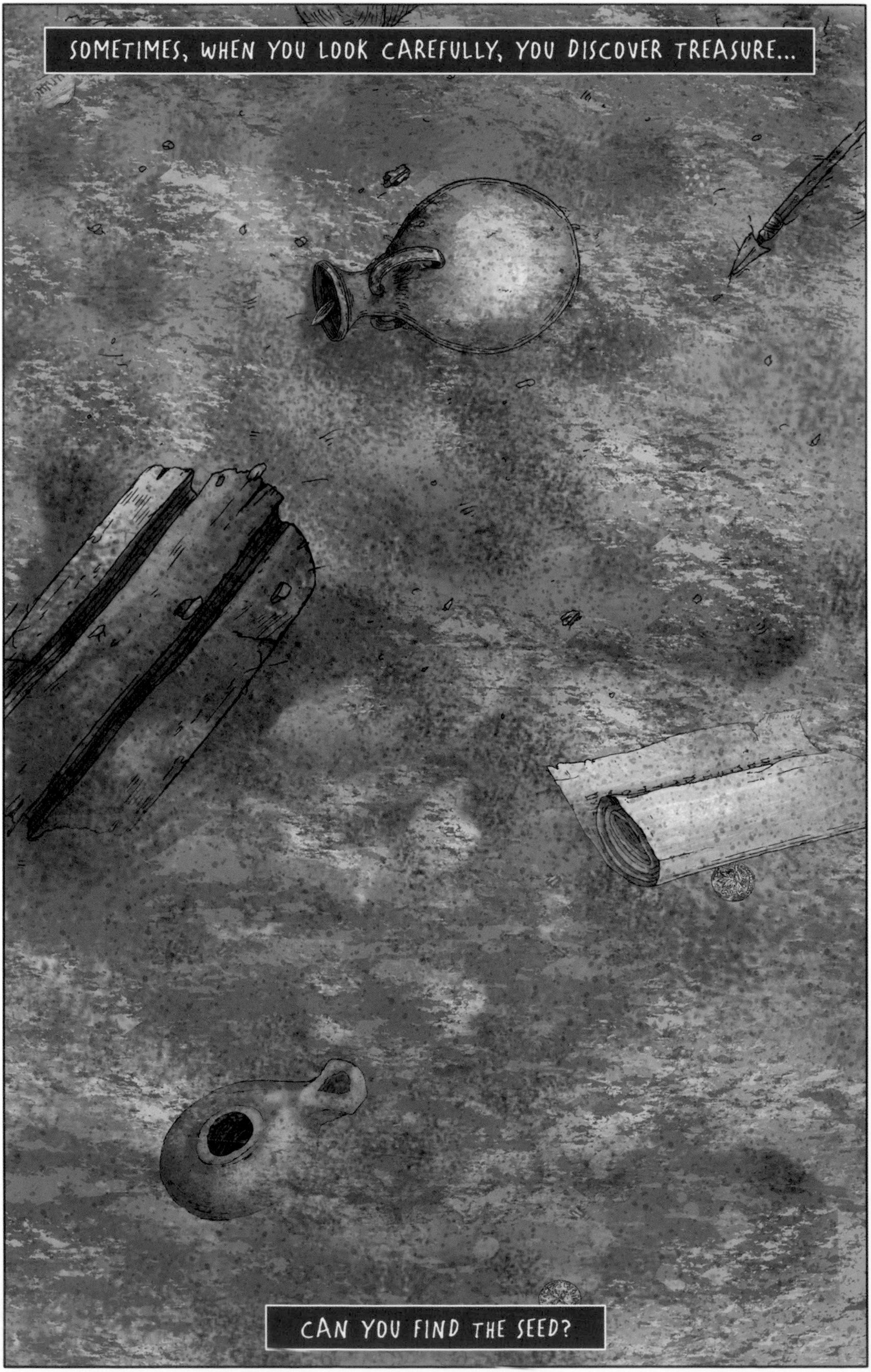
SOMETIMES, WHEN YOU LOOK CAREFULLY, YOU DISCOVER TREASURE...
CAN YOU FIND THE SEED?

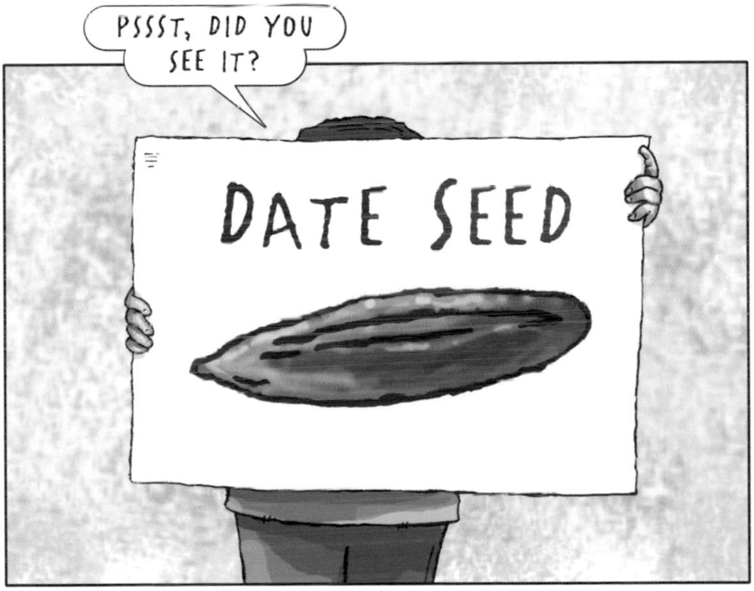
PSSST, DID YOU SEE IT?
DATE SEED

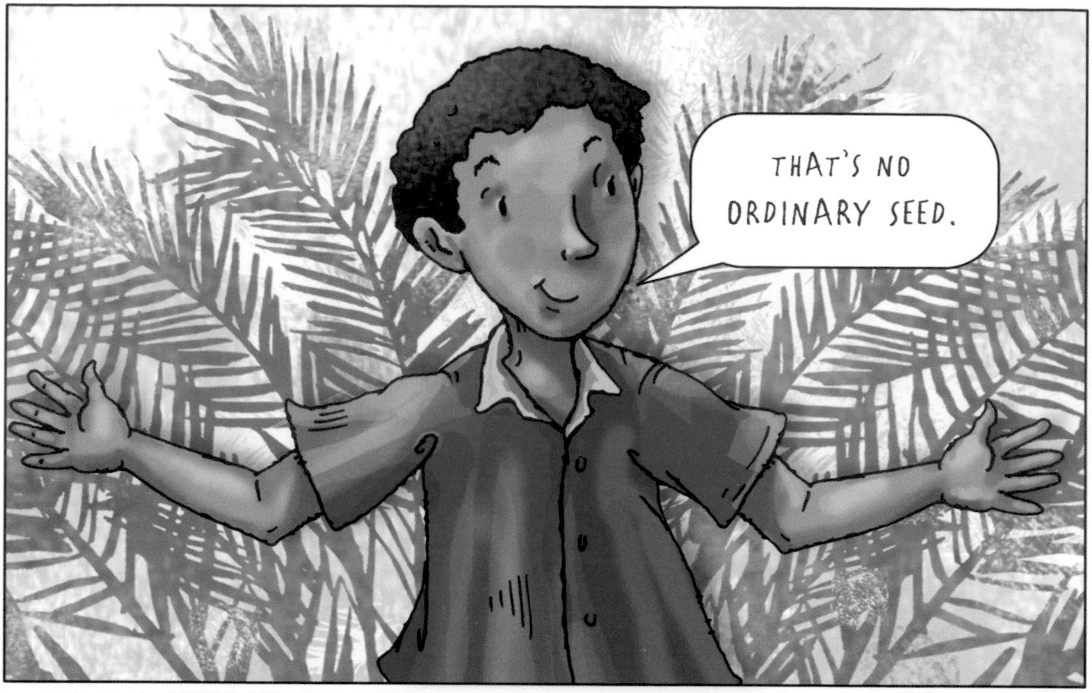
THAT'S NO ORDINARY SEED.

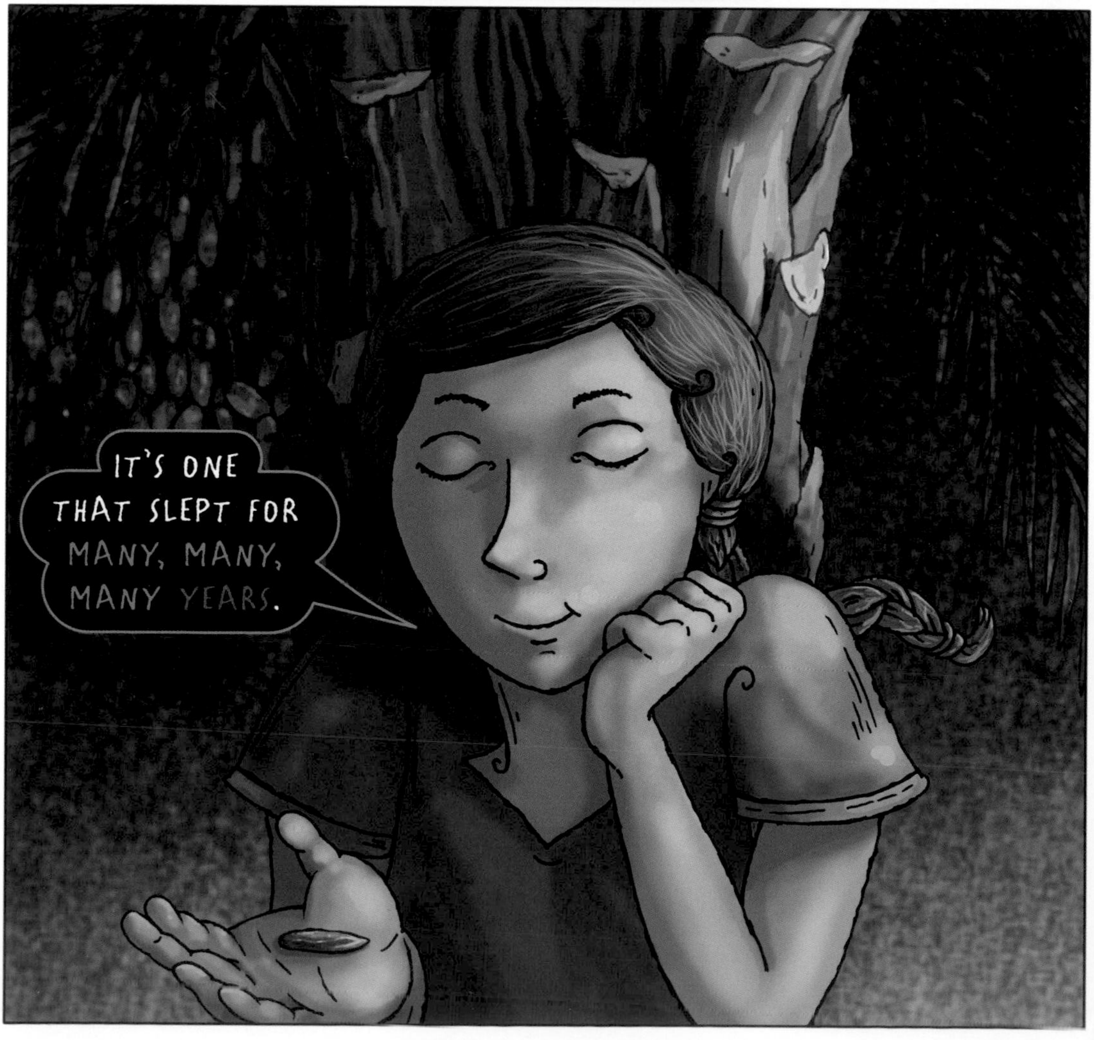
IT'S ONE THAT SLEPT FOR MANY, MANY, MANY YEARS.

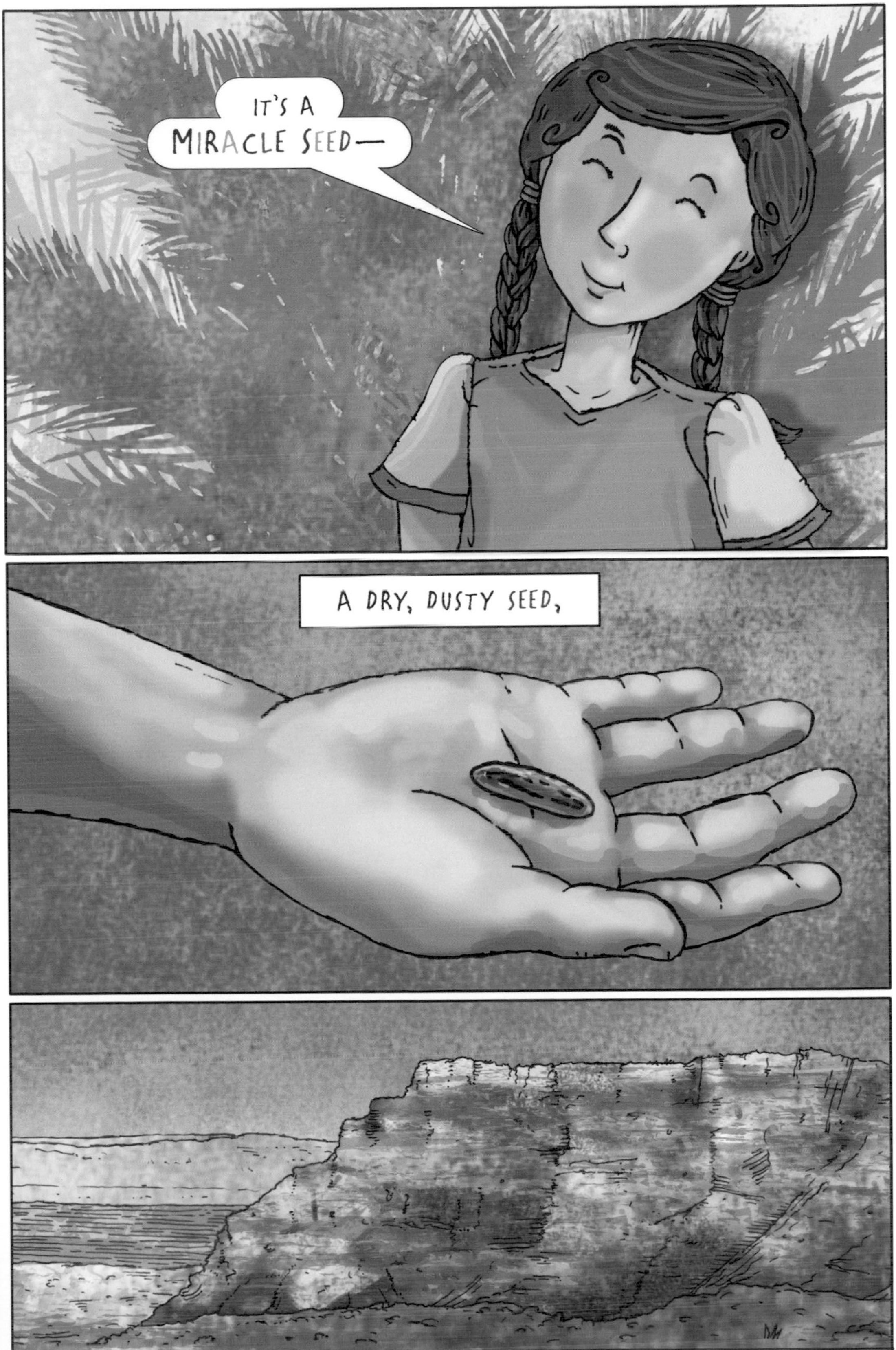
IT'S A MIRACLE SEED—
A DRY, DUSTY SEED,
THAT LAY BURIED IN SUN-BAKED DESERT SOIL, LOST FOR GENERATIONS.

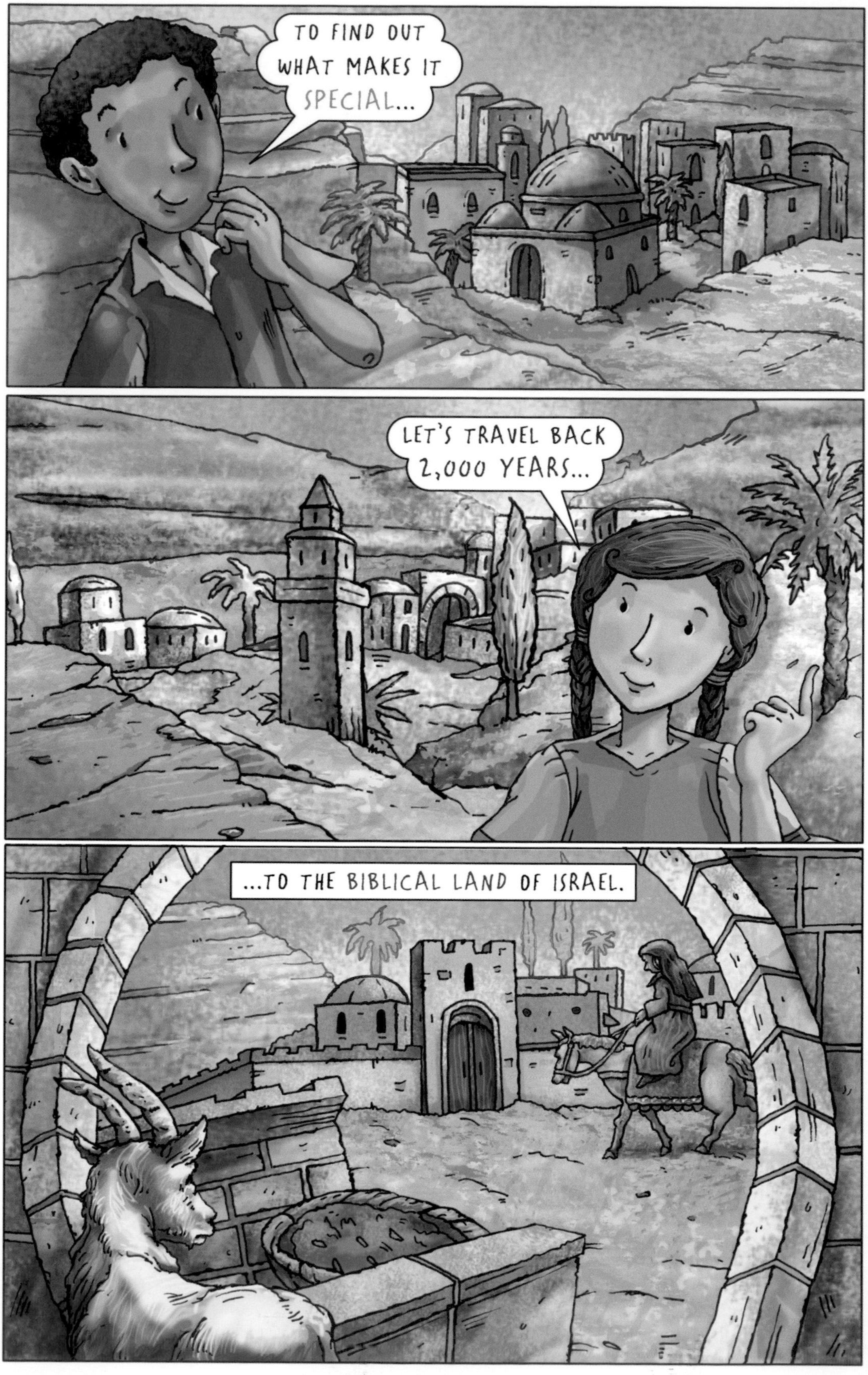
TO FIND OUT WHAT MAKES IT SPECIAL...
LET'S TRAVEL BACK 2,000 YEARS...
...TO THE BIBLICAL LAND OF ISRAEL.

PART
ONE
·REBELLION·

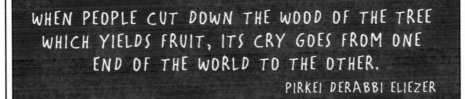

WHEN PEOPLE CUT DOWN THE WOOD OF THE TREE
WHICH YIELDS FRUIT, ITS CRY GOES FROM ONE
END OF THE WORLD TO THE OTHER.
                              PIRKEI DERABBI ELIEZER

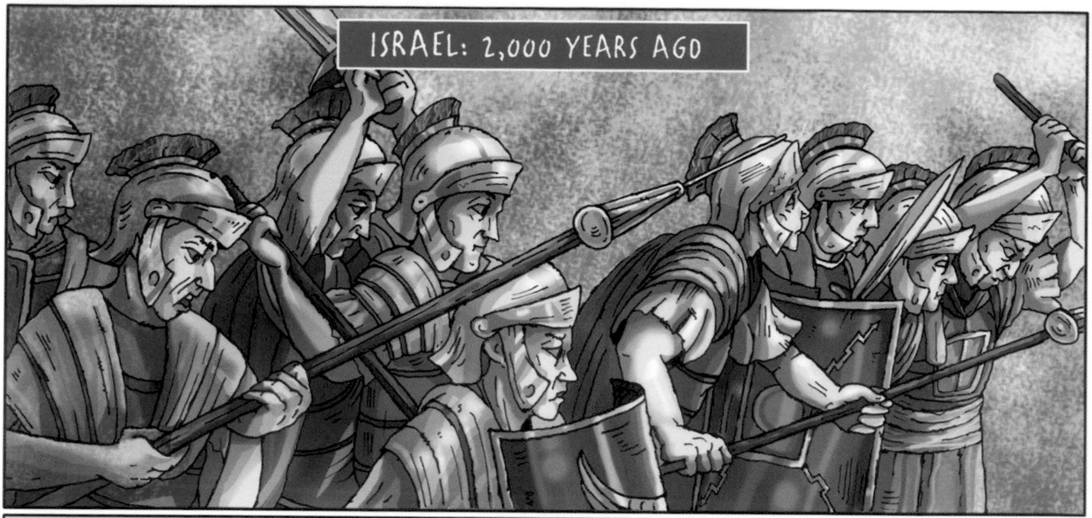
ISRAEL: 2,000 YEARS AGO

IT WAS A TIME OF REBELLION—A TIME WHEN THE JEWISH PEOPLE TOOK UP ARMS AGAINST THEIR ROMAN RULERS, IN HOPES OF BREAKING FREE FROM BRUTAL TYRANNY.

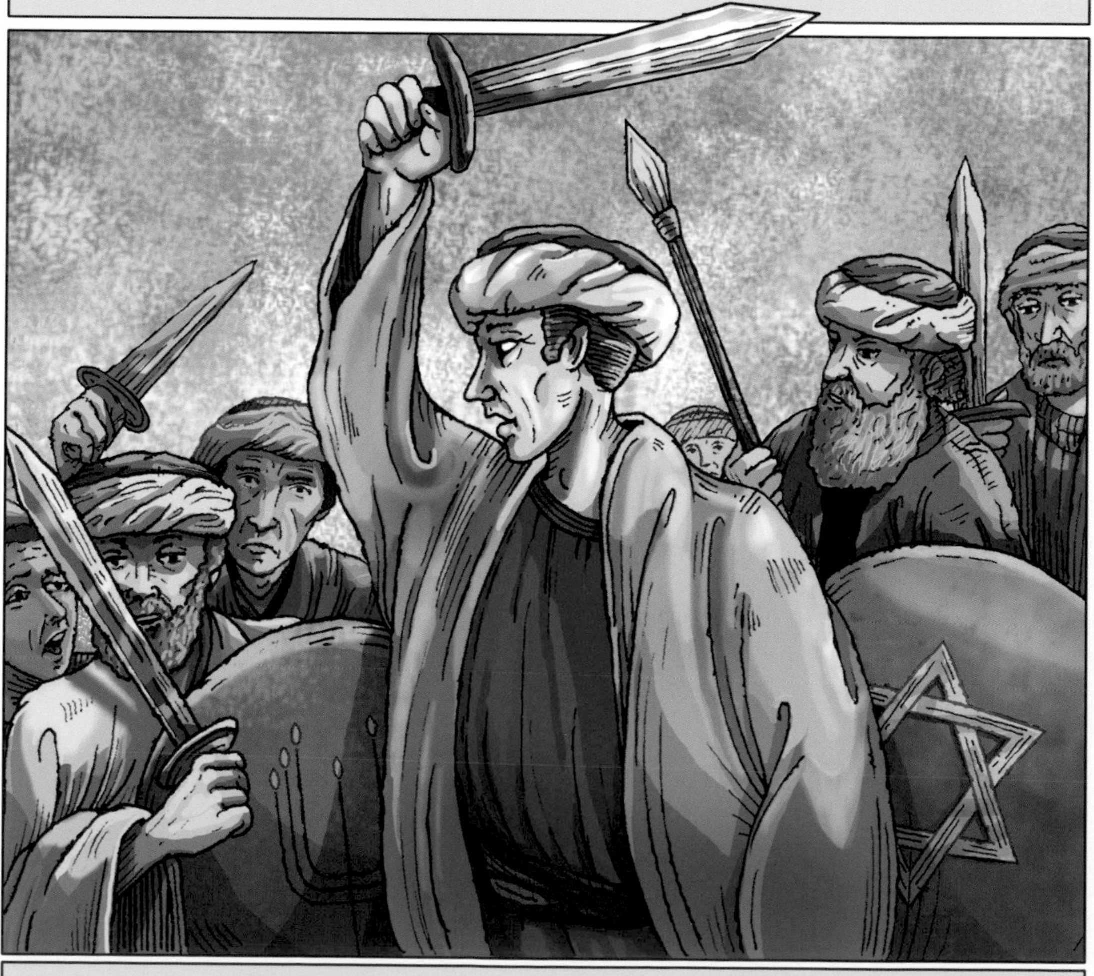

THEY FOUGHT WITH SPIRIT AND COURAGE.

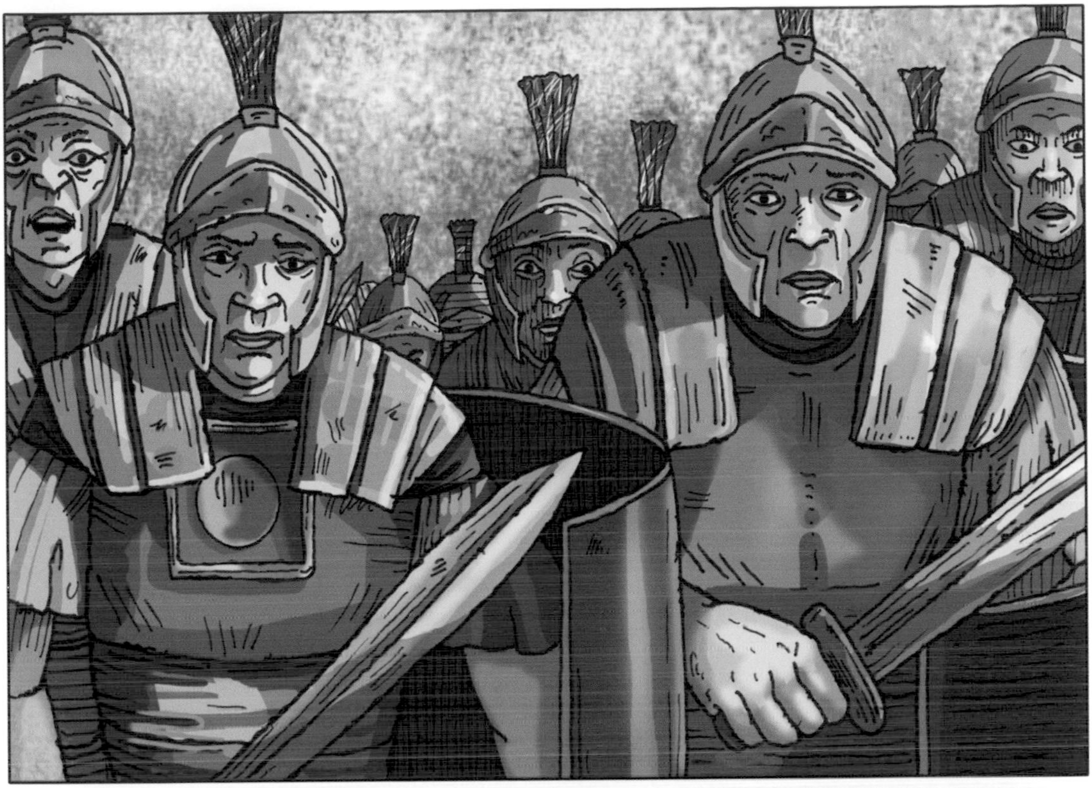

EMPEROR TITUS, THE ROMAN LEADER,
SENT THOUSANDS OF HIS BEST TROOPS TO CRUSH THE REVOLT.

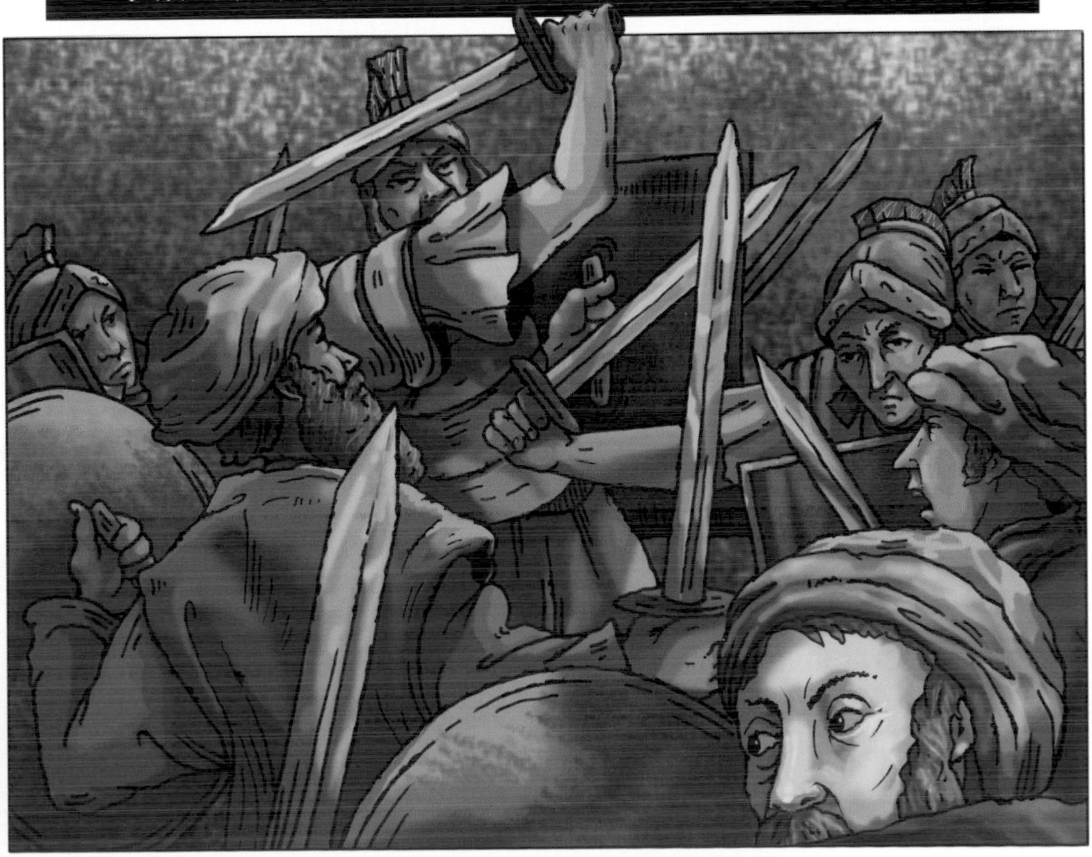

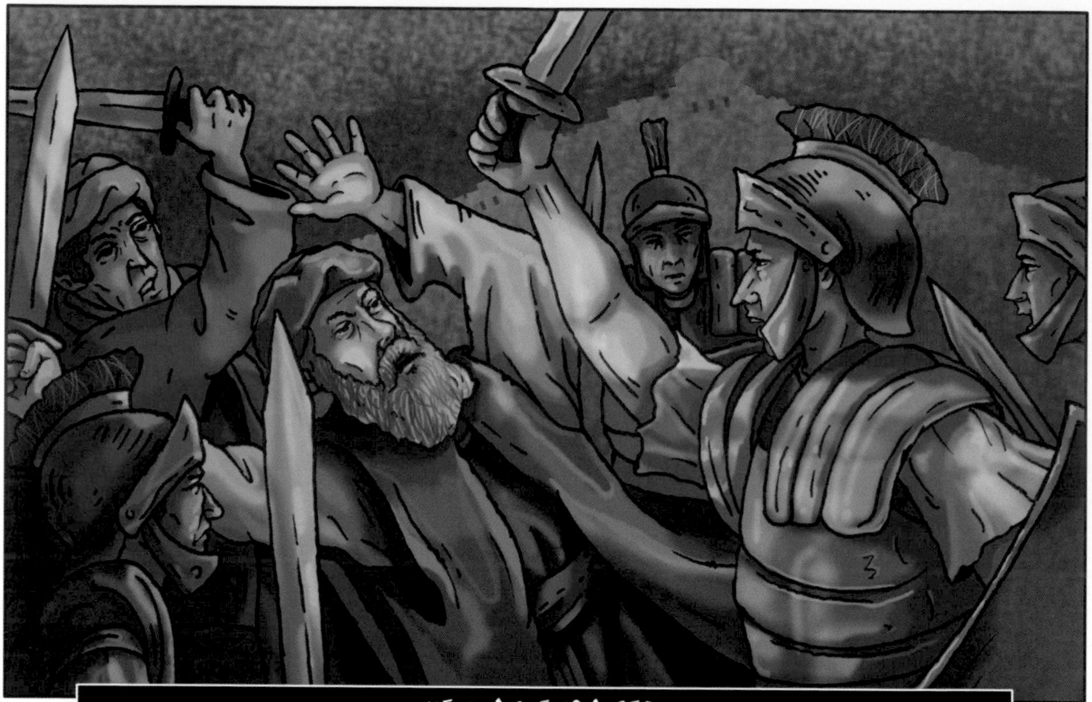

HE WAS ENRAGED.
HOW DARE THE JEWS CHALLENGE HIS MIGHTY ROMAN EMPIRE!

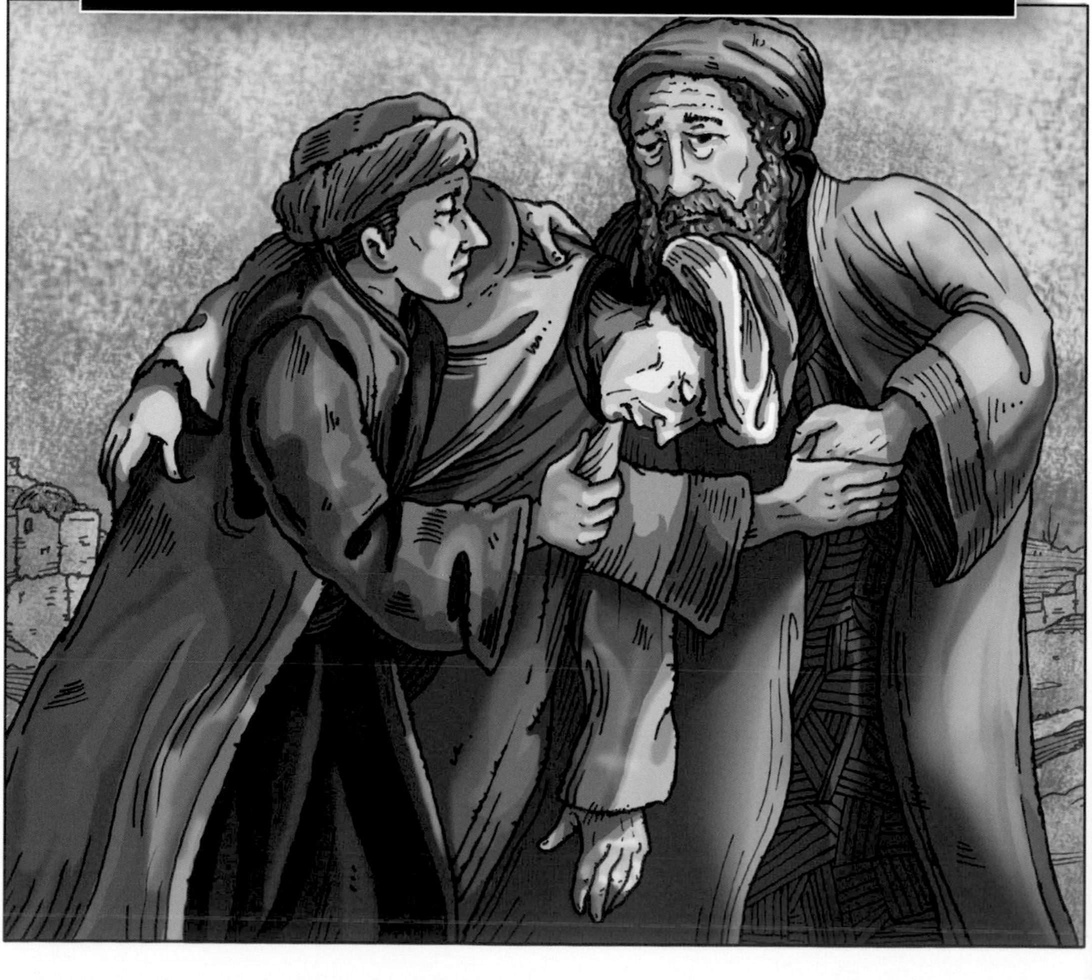

THE EMPEROR WAS COMMITTED TO CRUSHING THE UPRISING AND DESTROYING EVERYTHING THAT WAS PRECIOUS TO THE JEWS.

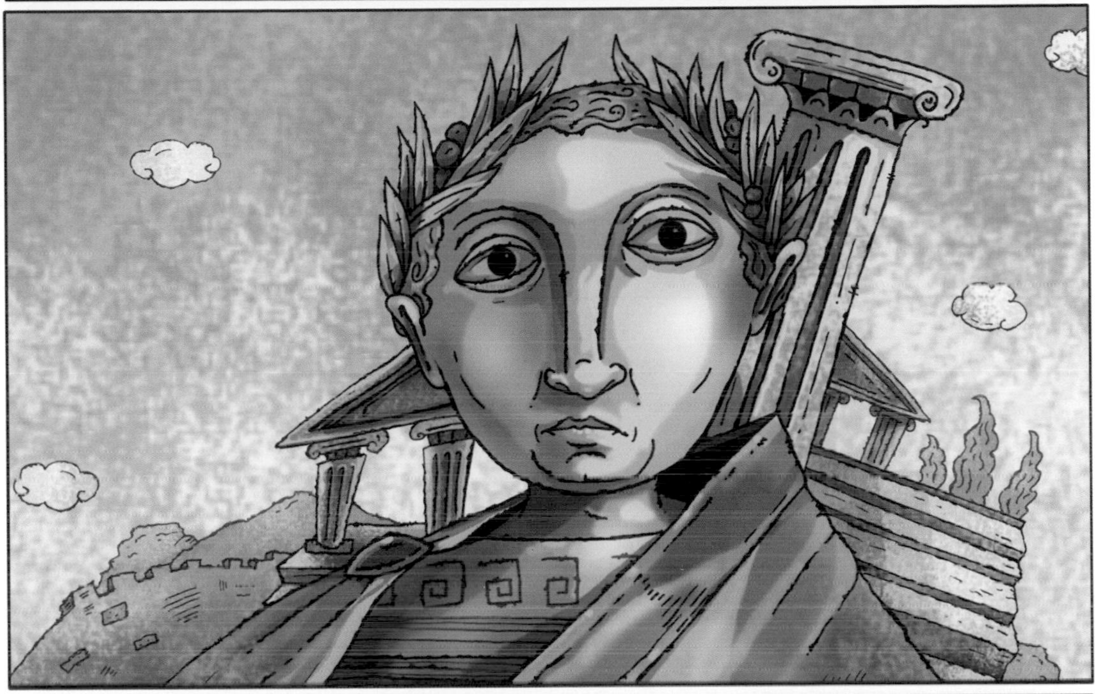

AFTER A TERRIBLE BATTLE, TITUS'S TROOPS STORMED THE WALLS OF JERUSALEM, ISRAEL'S CAPITAL, AND DEMOLISHED THE HOLY TEMPLE.

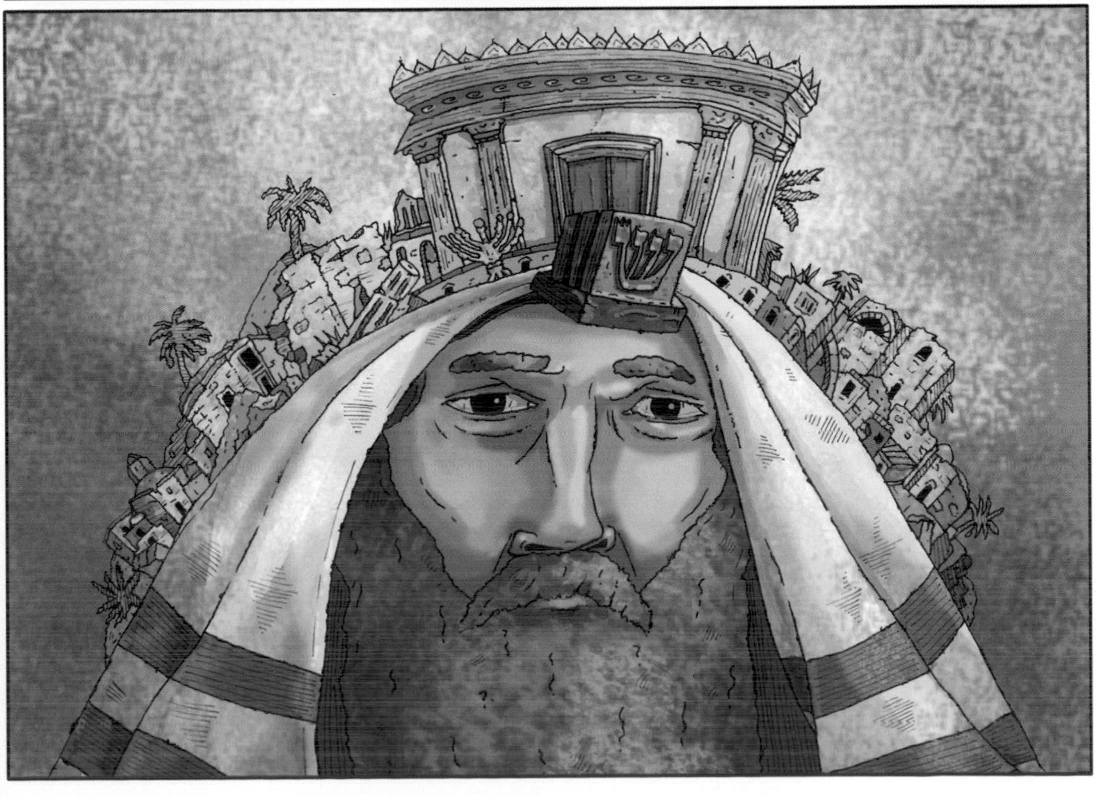

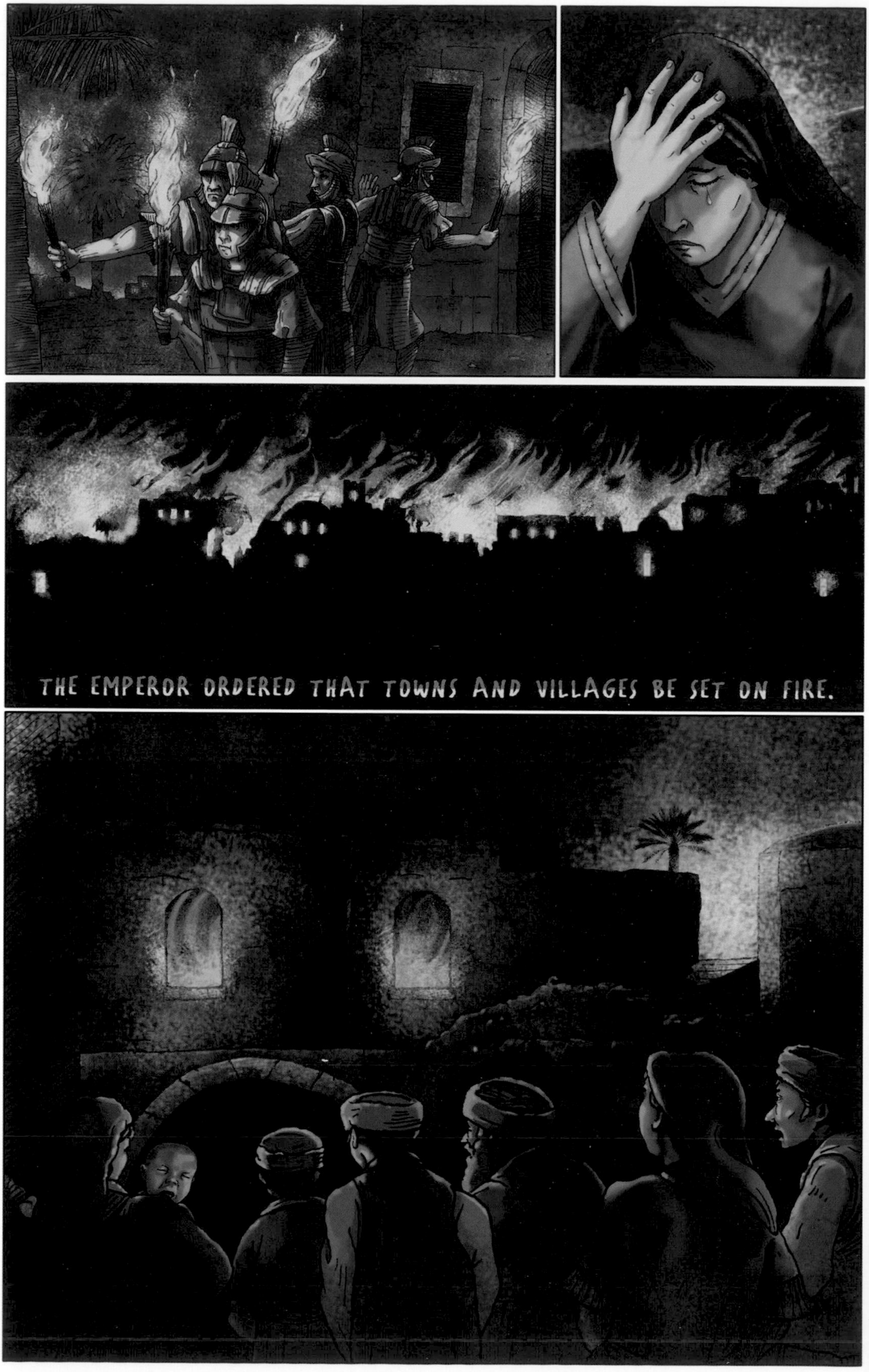
THE EMPEROR ORDERED THAT TOWNS AND VILLAGES BE SET ON FIRE.

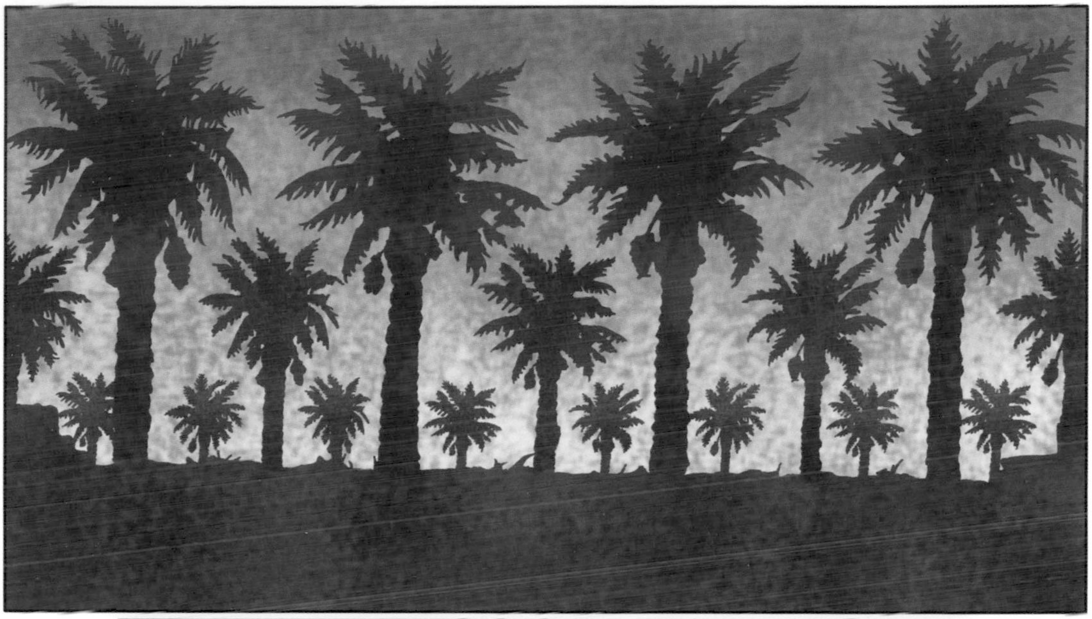

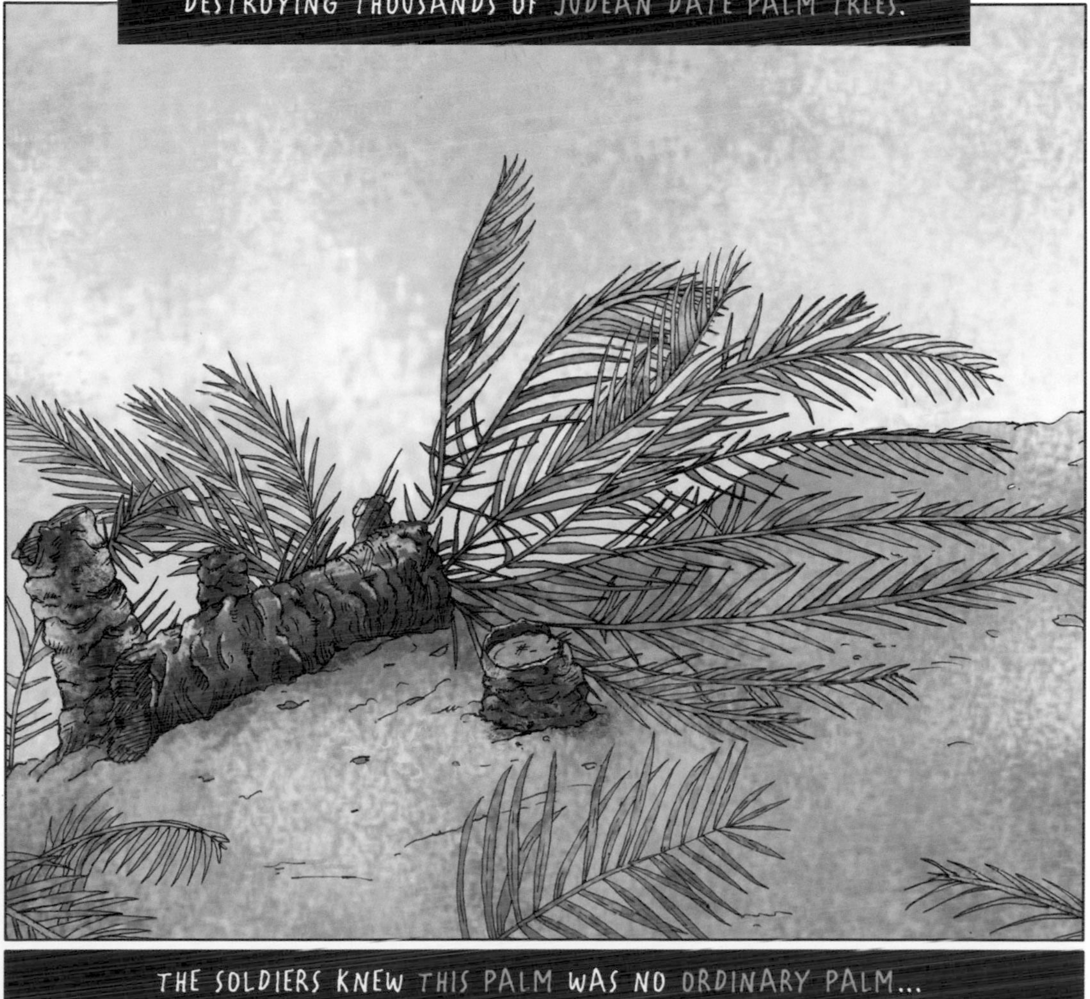
HORDES OF ROMAN SOLDIERS TRAVELED THROUGHOUT THE LAND, DESTROYING THOUSANDS OF JUDEAN DATE PALM TREES.
THE SOLDIERS KNEW THIS PALM WAS NO ORDINARY PALM...

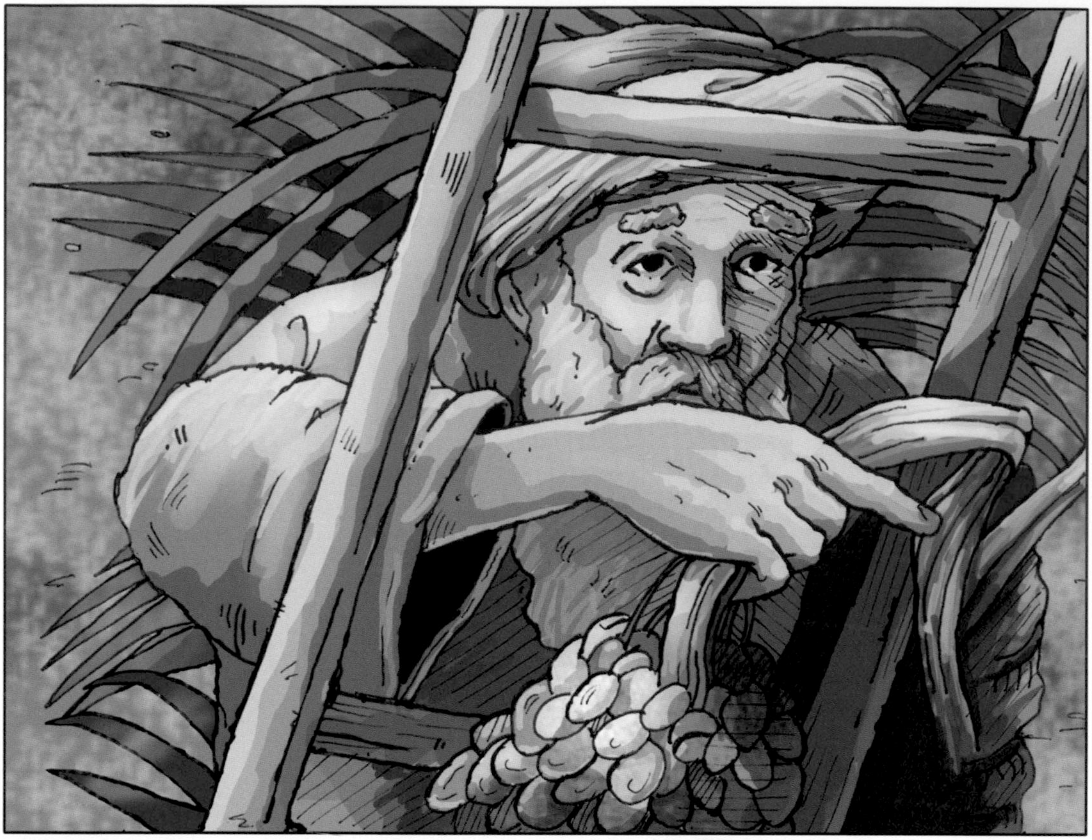

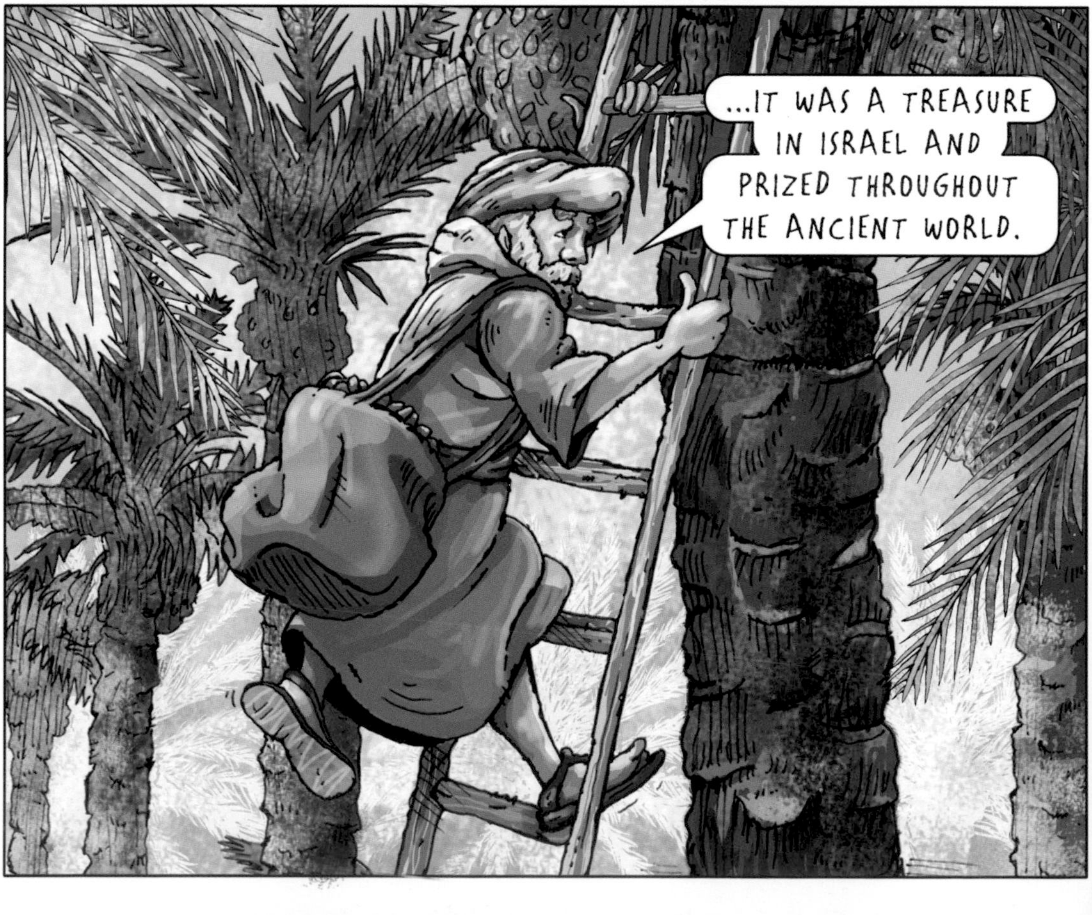
...IT WAS A TREASURE IN ISRAEL AND PRIZED THROUGHOUT THE ANCIENT WORLD.

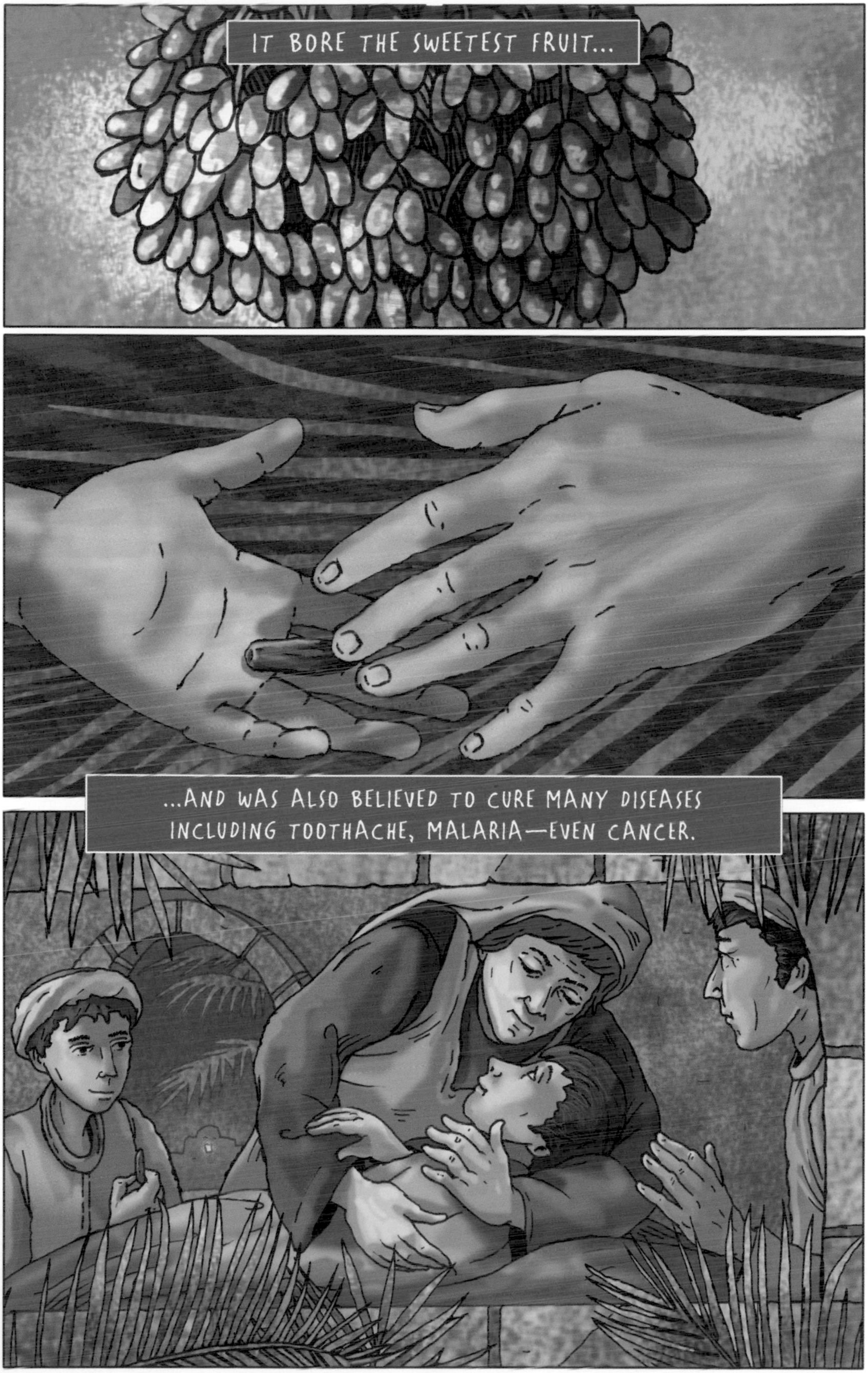
IT BORE THE SWEETEST FRUIT...
...AND WAS ALSO BELIEVED TO CURE MANY DISEASES INCLUDING TOOTHACHE, MALARIA—EVEN CANCER.

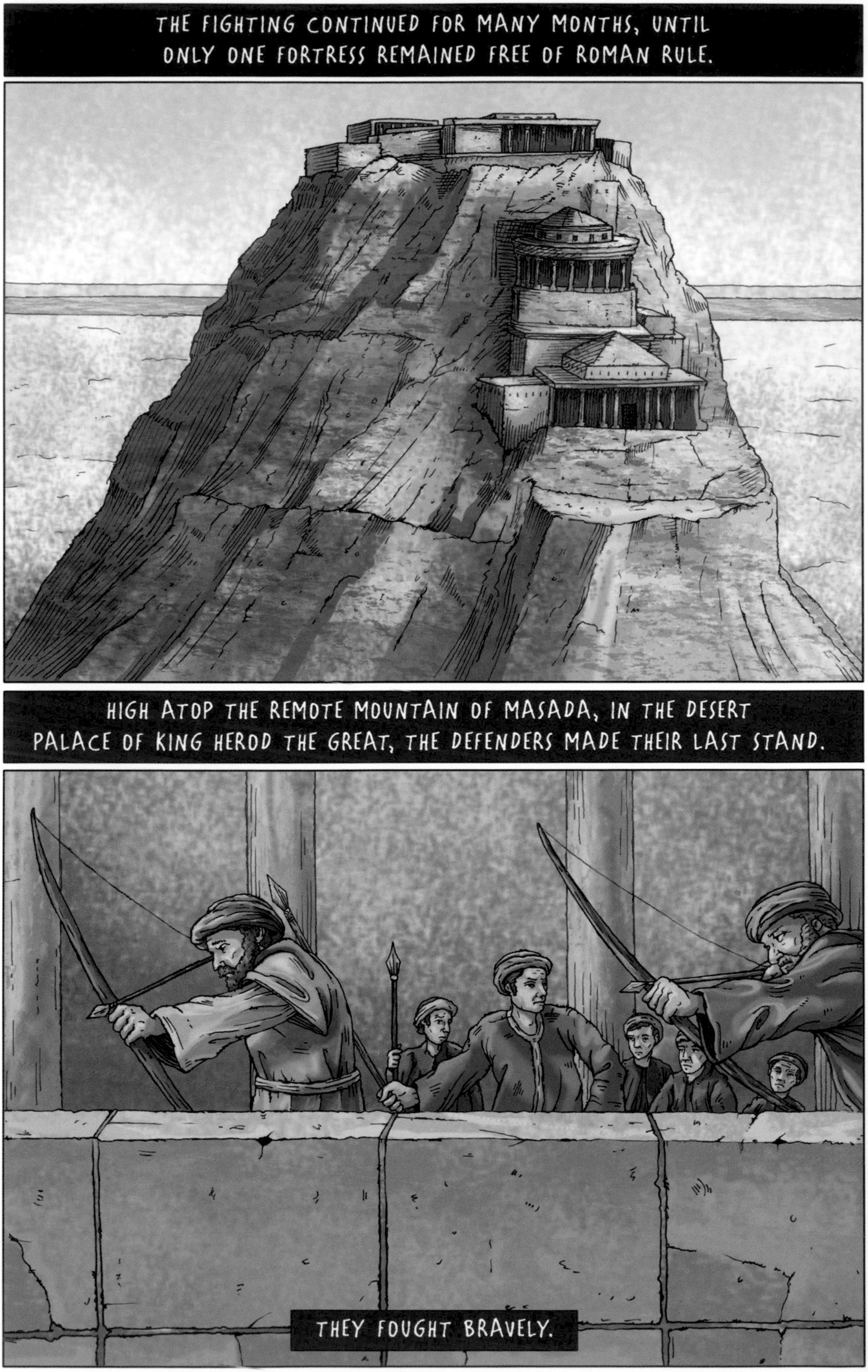
THE FIGHTING CONTINUED FOR MANY MONTHS, UNTIL ONLY ONE FORTRESS REMAINED FREE OF ROMAN RULE.
HIGH ATOP THE REMOTE MOUNTAIN OF MASADA, IN THE DESERT PALACE OF KING HEROD THE GREAT, THE DEFENDERS MADE THEIR LAST STAND.
THEY FOUGHT BRAVELY.

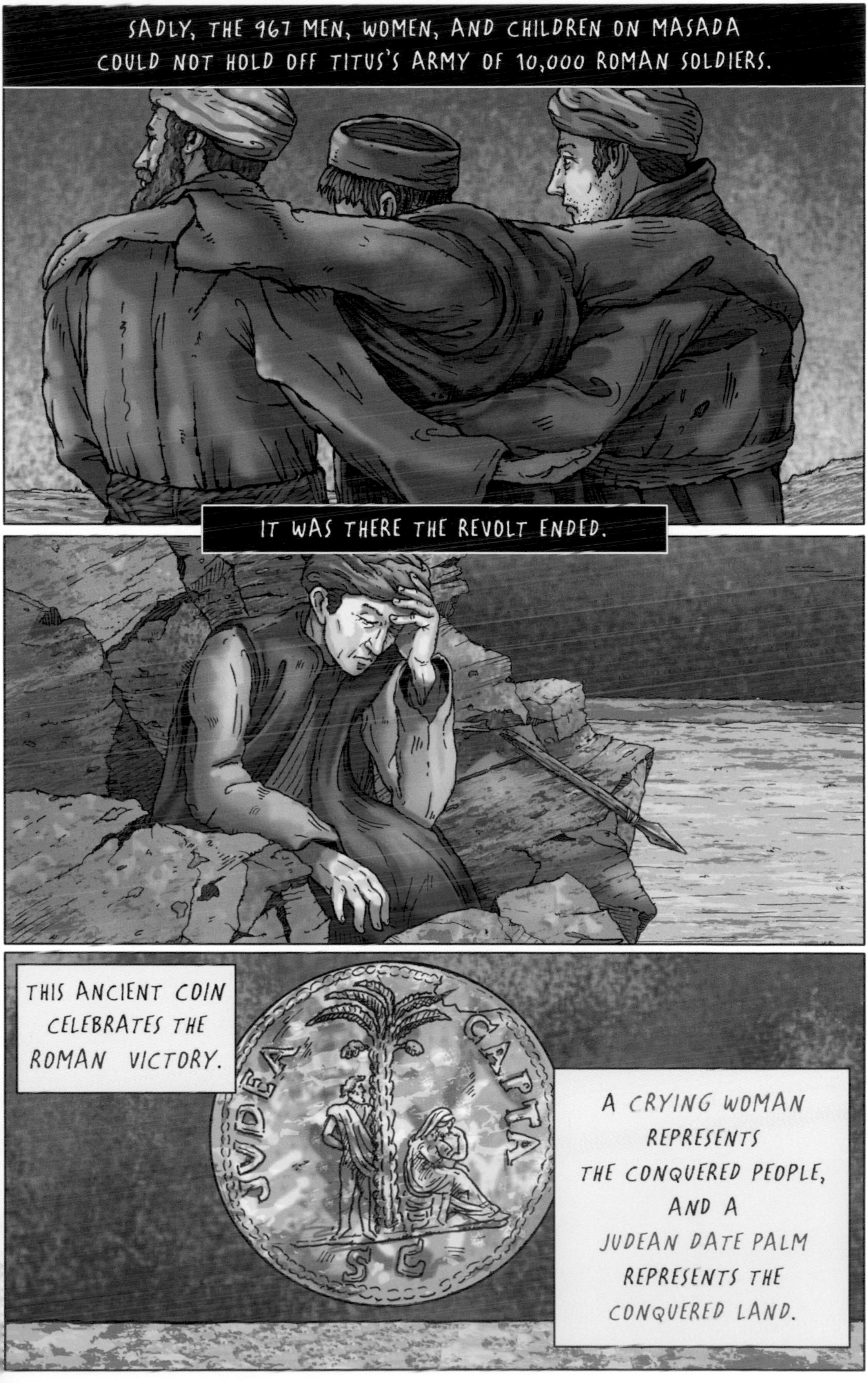
SADLY, THE 967 MEN, WOMEN, AND CHILDREN ON MASADA COULD NOT HOLD OFF TITUS'S ARMY OF 10,000 ROMAN SOLDIERS.
IT WAS THERE THE REVOLT ENDED.
THIS ANCIENT COIN CELEBRATES THE ROMAN VICTORY.
JUDEA CAPTA
S C
A CRYING WOMAN REPRESENTS THE CONQUERED PEOPLE, AND A JUDEAN DATE PALM REPRESENTS THE CONQUERED LAND.

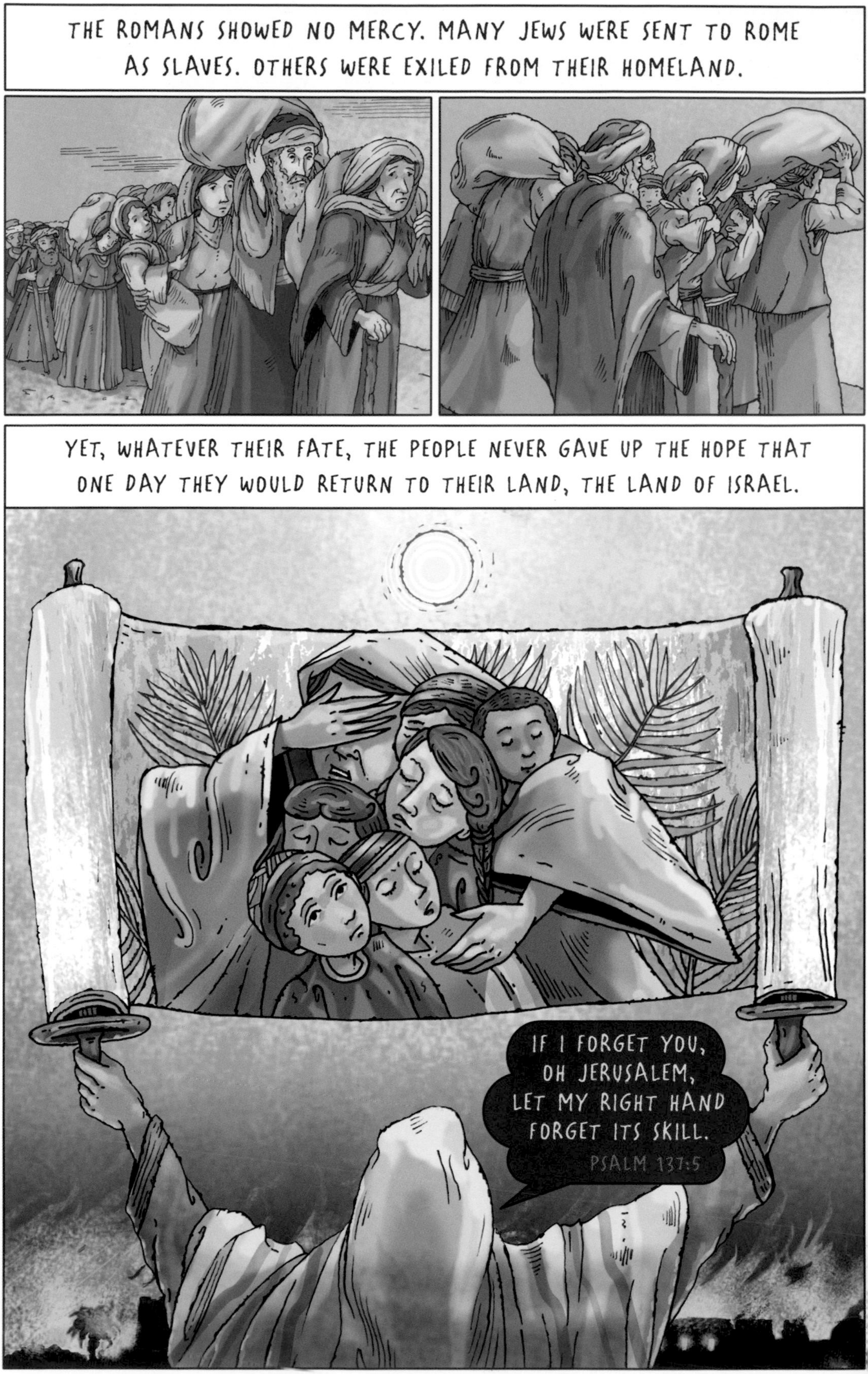
THE ROMANS SHOWED NO MERCY. MANY JEWS WERE SENT TO ROME AS SLAVES. OTHERS WERE EXILED FROM THEIR HOMELAND.
YET, WHATEVER THEIR FATE, THE PEOPLE NEVER GAVE UP THE HOPE THAT ONE DAY THEY WOULD RETURN TO THEIR LAND, THE LAND OF ISRAEL.
IF I FORGET YOU, OH JERUSALEM, LET MY RIGHT HAND FORGET ITS SKILL.
PSALM 137:5

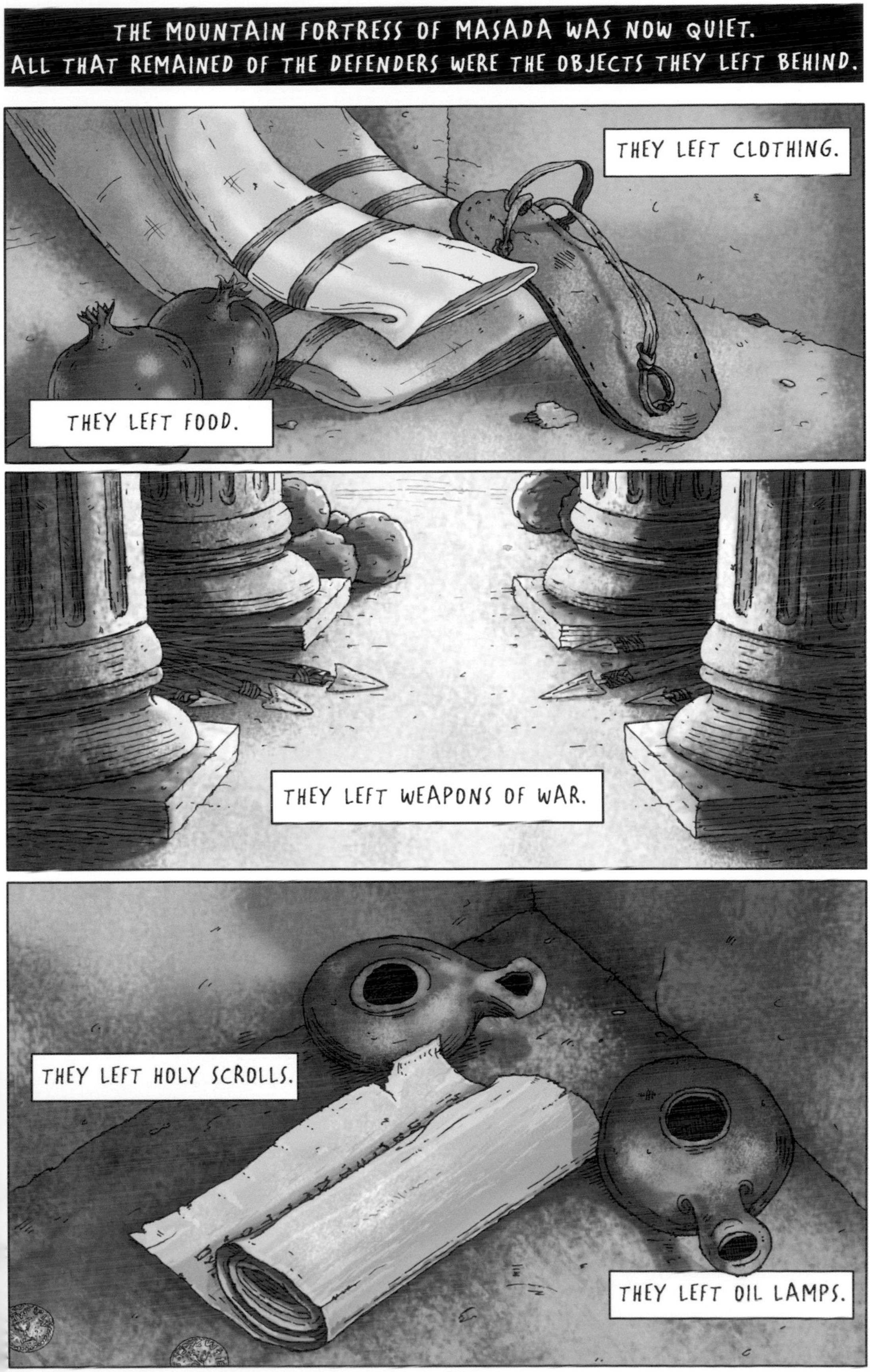
THE MOUNTAIN FORTRESS OF MASADA WAS NOW QUIET.
ALL THAT REMAINED OF THE DEFENDERS WERE THE OBJECTS THEY LEFT BEHIND.
THEY LEFT CLOTHING.
THEY LEFT FOOD.
THEY LEFT WEAPONS OF WAR.
THEY LEFT HOLY SCROLLS.
THEY LEFT OIL LAMPS.

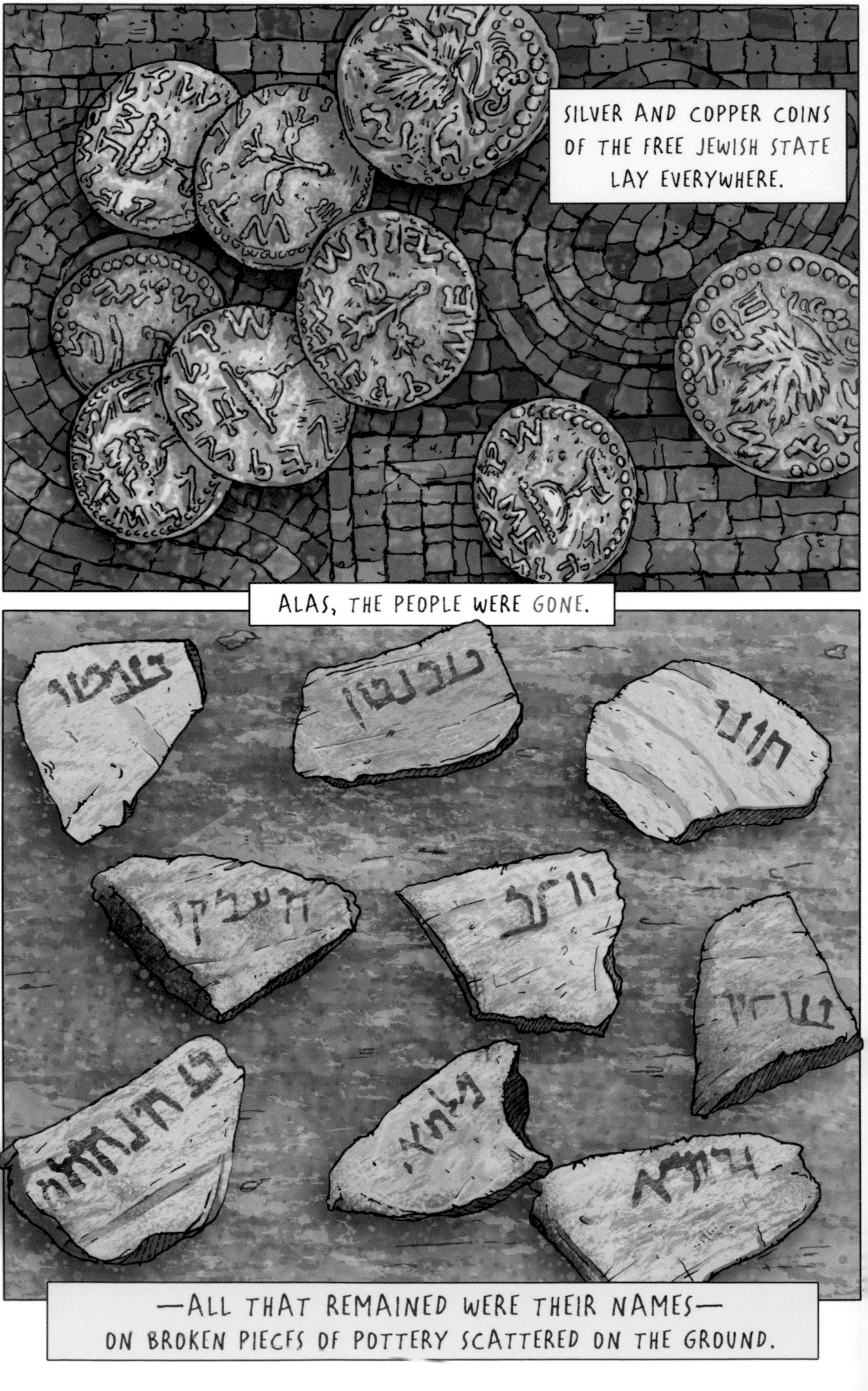
SILVER AND COPPER COINS OF THE FREE JEWISH STATE LAY EVERYWHERE.
ALAS, THE PEOPLE WERE GONE.
—ALL THAT REMAINED WERE THEIR NAMES—
ON BROKEN PIECES OF POTTERY SCATTERED ON THE GROUND.

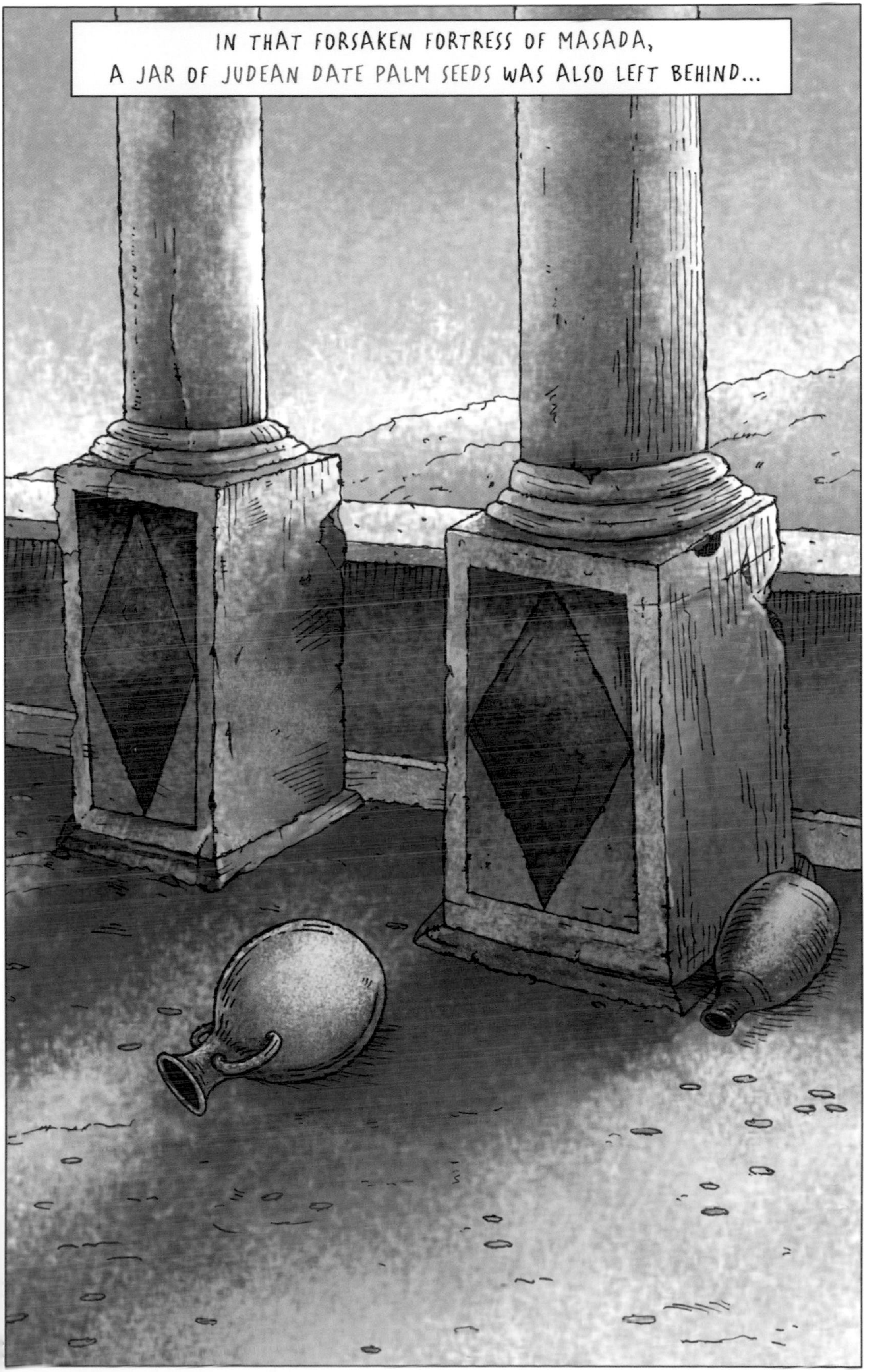
IN THAT FORSAKEN FORTRESS OF MASADA,
A JAR OF JUDEAN DATE PALM SEEDS WAS ALSO LEFT BEHIND...

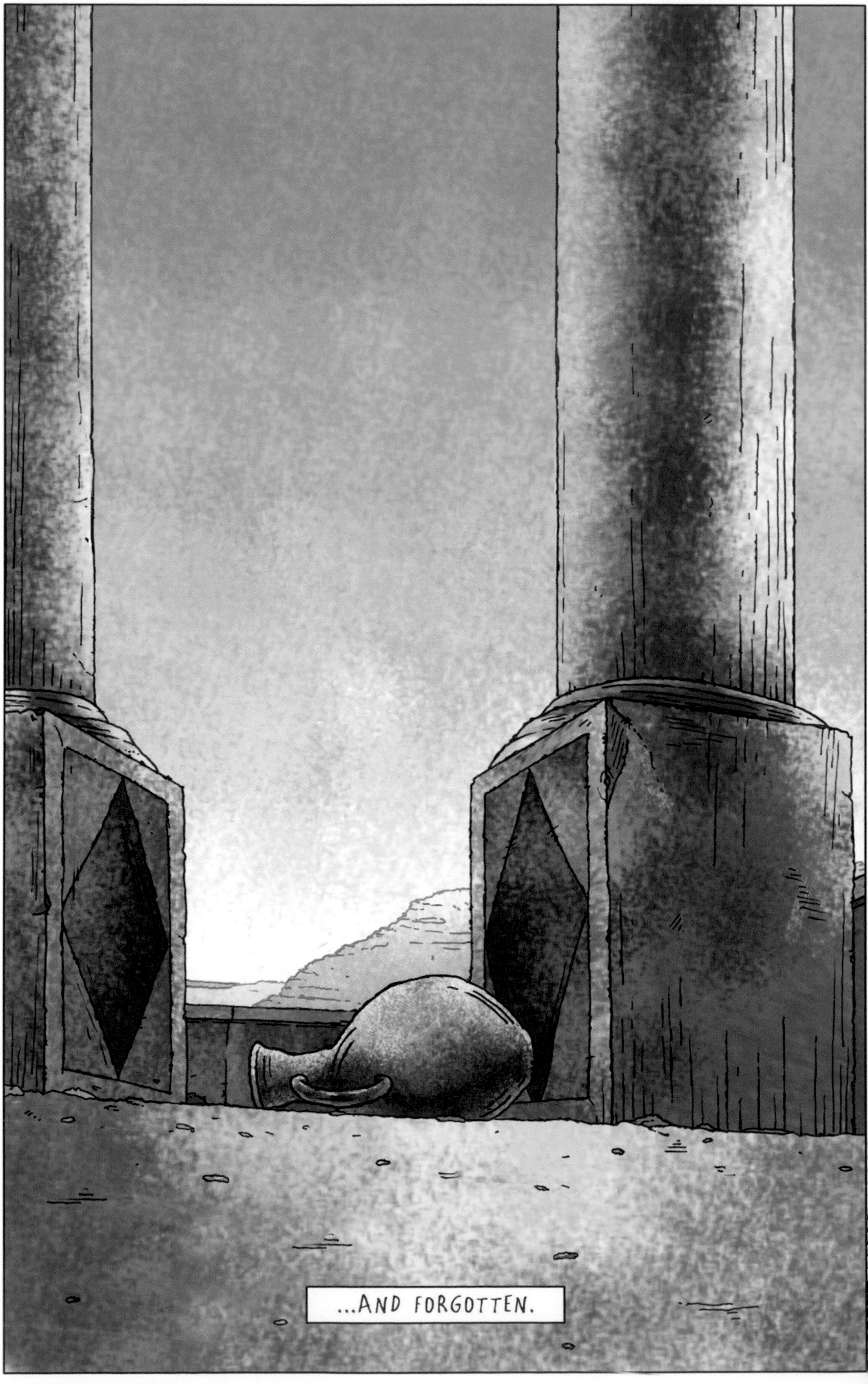
...AND FORGOTTEN.

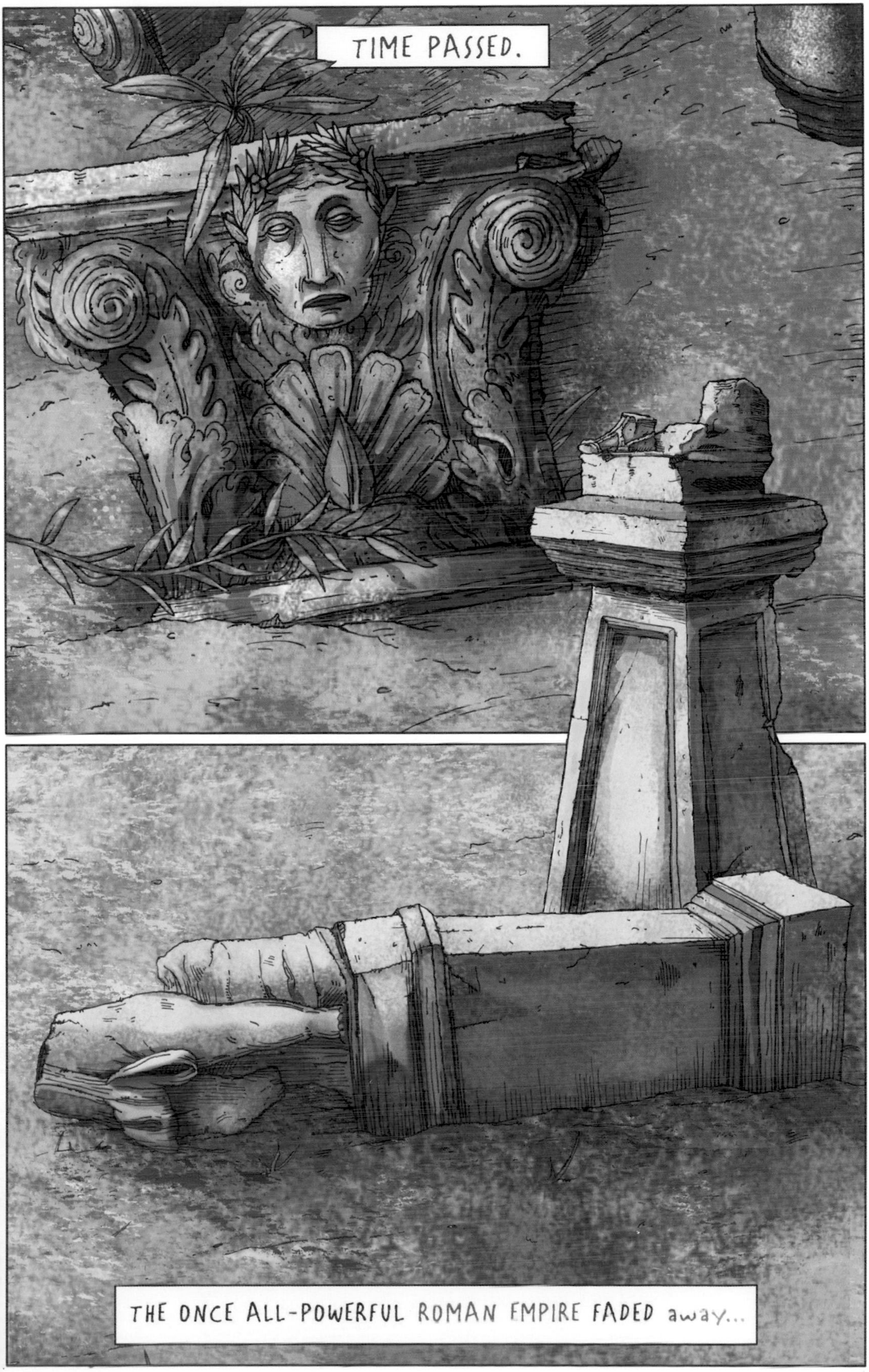
TIME PASSED.
THE ONCE ALL-POWERFUL ROMAN EMPIRE FADED away...

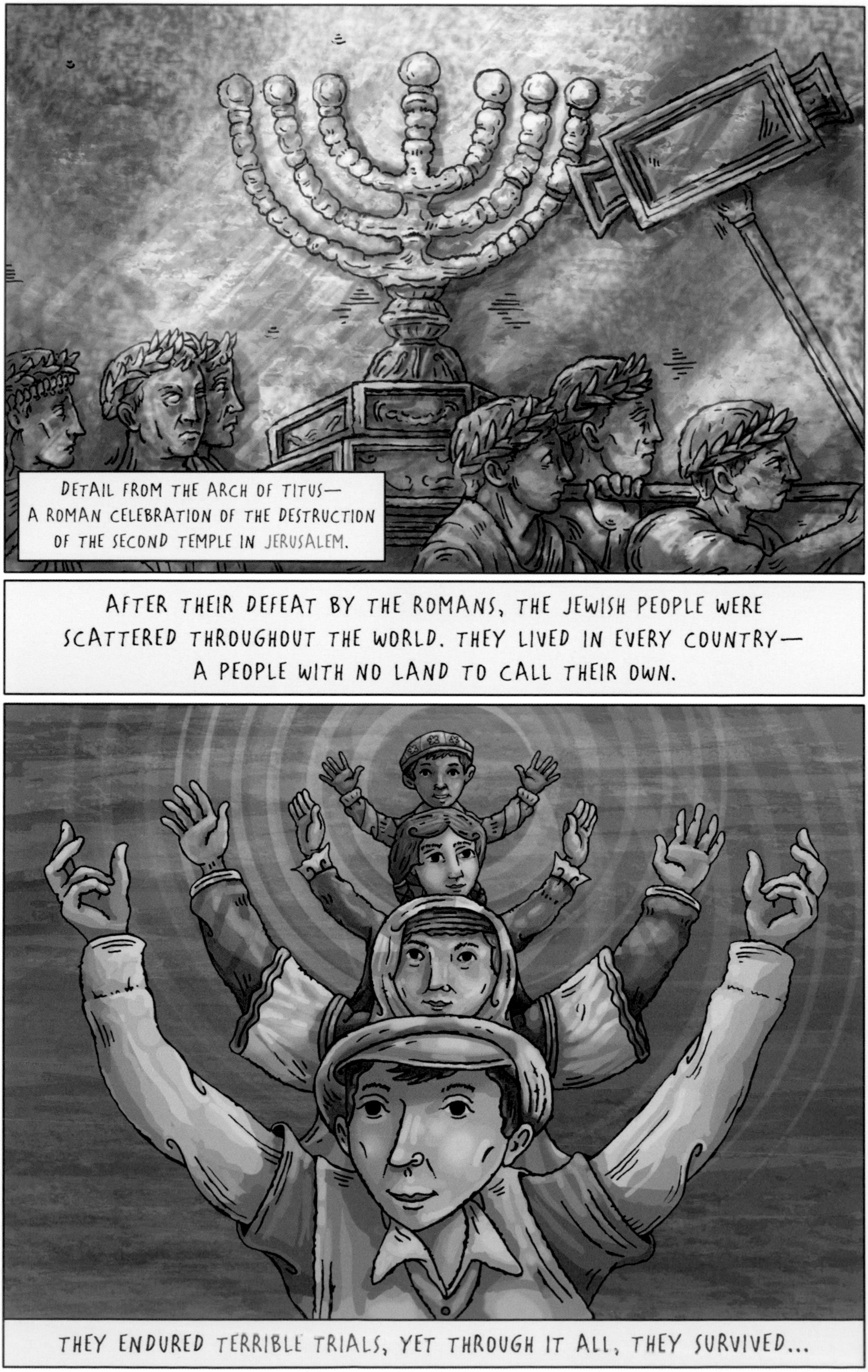
DETAIL FROM THE ARCH OF TITUS—A ROMAN CELEBRATION OF THE DESTRUCTION OF THE SECOND TEMPLE IN JERUSALEM.
AFTER THEIR DEFEAT BY THE ROMANS, THE JEWISH PEOPLE WERE SCATTERED THROUGHOUT THE WORLD. THEY LIVED IN EVERY COUNTRY—A PEOPLE WITH NO LAND TO CALL THEIR OWN.
THEY ENDURED TERRIBLE TRIALS, YET THROUGH IT ALL, THEY SURVIVED...

PART
TWO
·HOPE·

LOOK DEEP INTO NATURE AND THEN YOU
WILL UNDERSTAND EVERYTHING BETTER.

ALBERT EINSTEIN

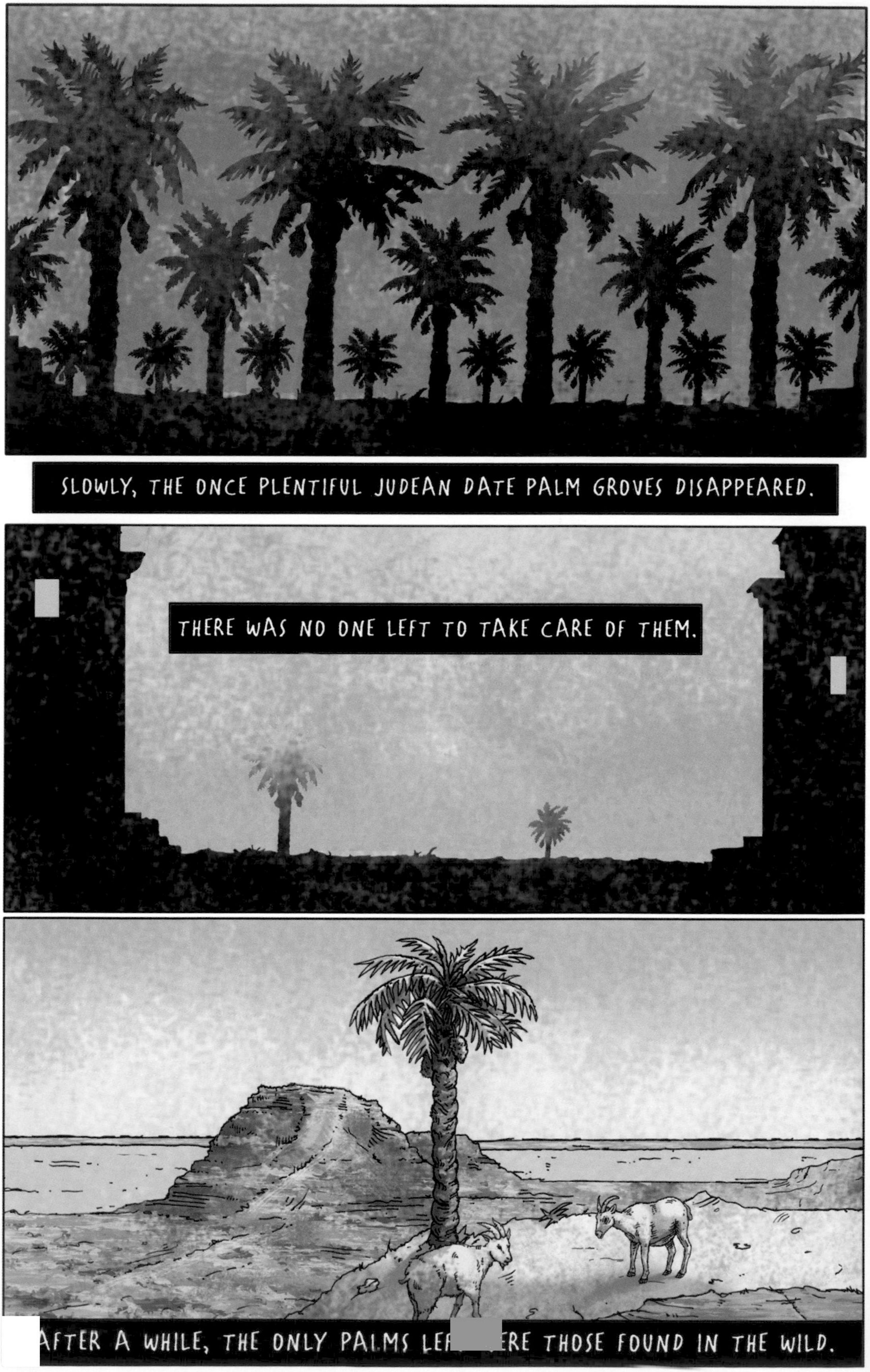
SLOWLY, THE ONCE PLENTIFUL JUDEAN DATE PALM GROVES DISAPPEARED.
THERE WAS NO ONE LEFT TO TAKE CARE OF THEM.
AFTER A WHILE, THE ONLY PALMS LEF ERE THOSE FOUND IN THE WILD.

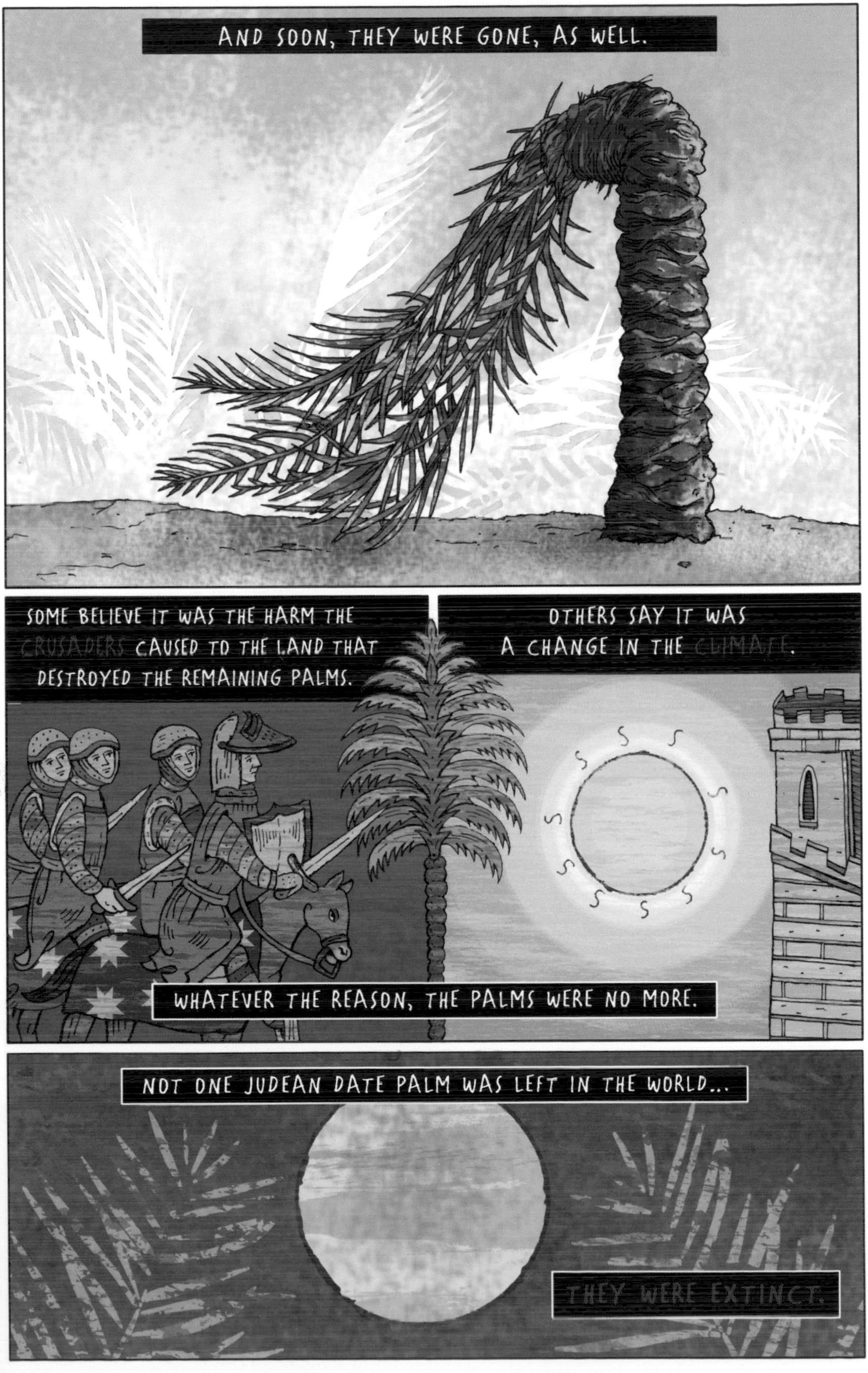

AND SOON, THEY WERE GONE, AS WELL.
SOME BELIEVE IT WAS THE HARM THE CRUSADERS CAUSED TO THE LAND THAT DESTROYED THE REMAINING PALMS.
OTHERS SAY IT WAS A CHANGE IN THE CLIMATE.
WHATEVER THE REASON, THE PALMS WERE NO MORE.
NOT ONE JUDEAN DATE PALM WAS LEFT IN THE WORLD...
THEY WERE EXTINCT.

DAY AFTER DAY. YEAR AFTER YEAR. CENTURY AFTER CENTURY...
THE EARTH SPUN IN AND OUT OF SEASONS.

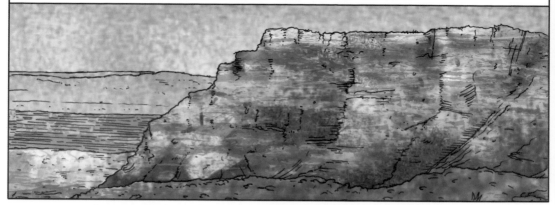

A HOT, DRY WIND BLEW THROUGH THE RUINS OF MASADA.

BRICKS AND STONES FELL TO THE GROUND.

SAND COVERED EVERYTHING.

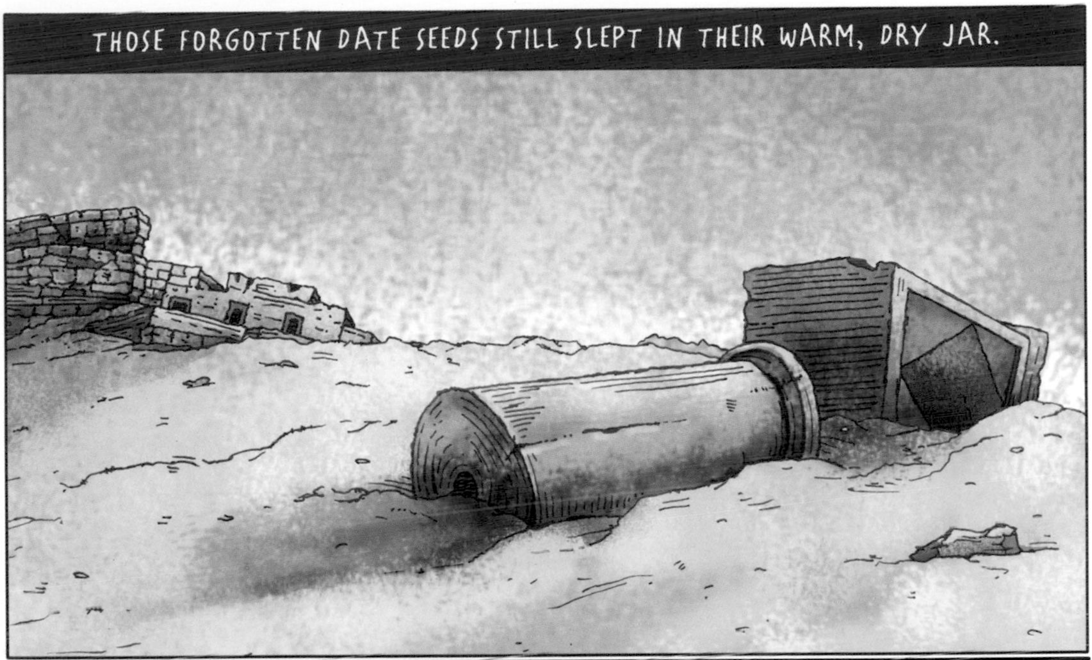
THOSE FORGOTTEN DATE SEEDS STILL SLEPT IN THEIR WARM, DRY JAR.

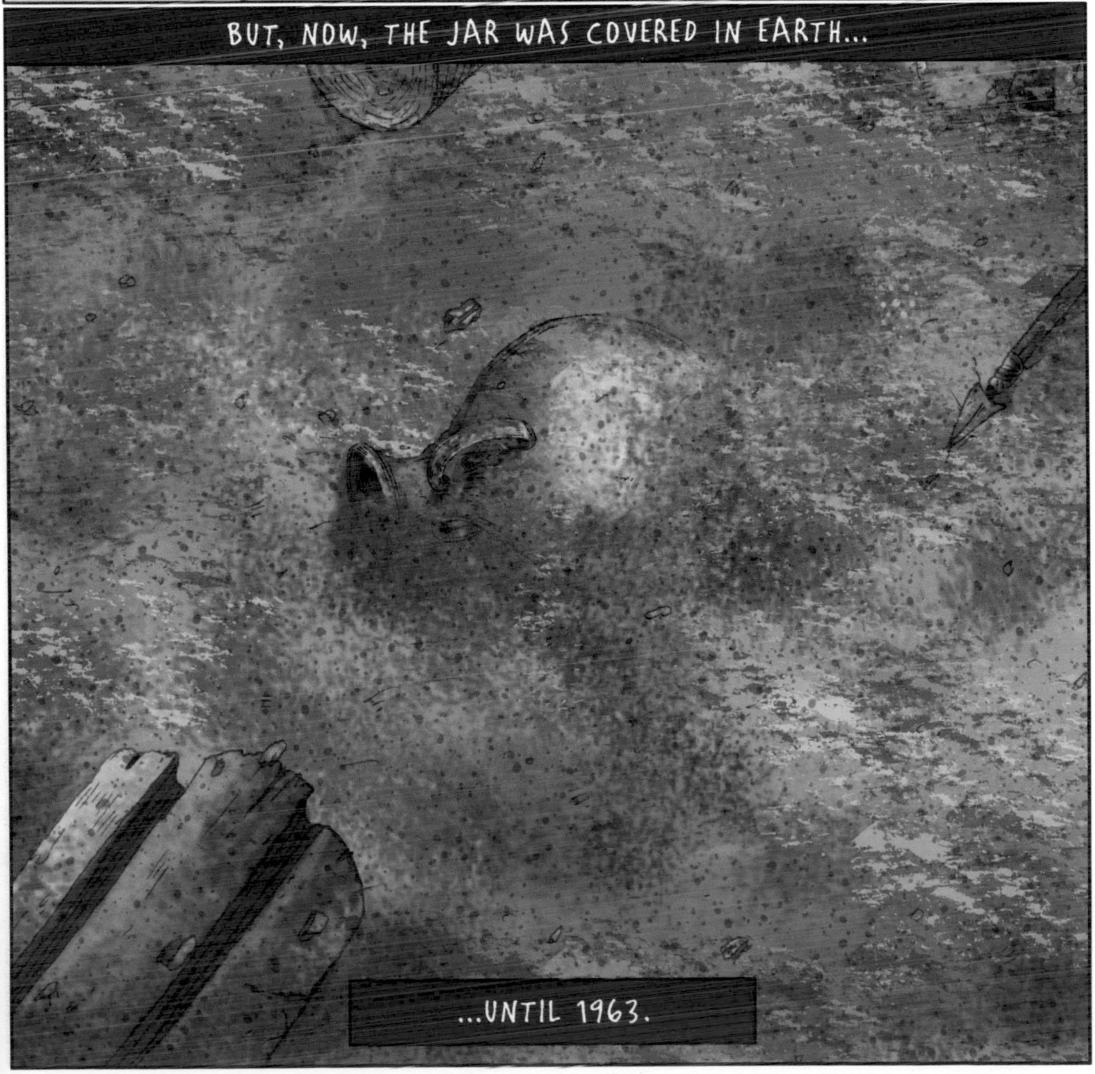
BUT, NOW, THE JAR WAS COVERED IN EARTH...
...UNTIL 1963.

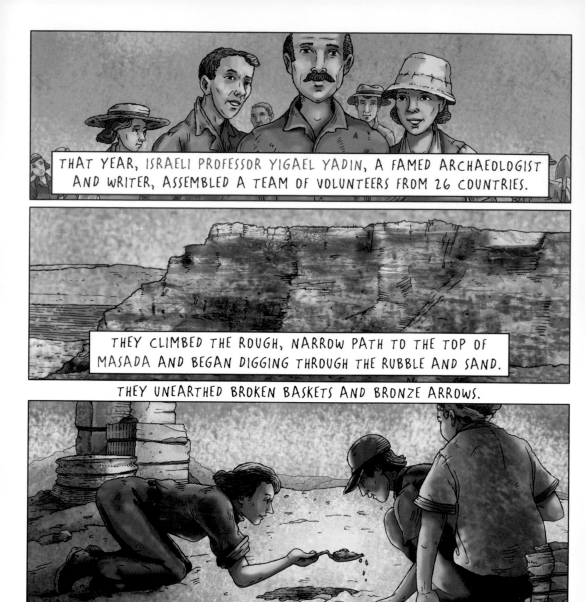

THAT YEAR, ISRAELI PROFESSOR YIGAEL YADIN, A FAMED ARCHAEOLOGIST AND WRITER, ASSEMBLED A TEAM OF VOLUNTEERS FROM 26 COUNTRIES.

THEY CLIMBED THE ROUGH, NARROW PATH TO THE TOP OF MASADA AND BEGAN DIGGING THROUGH THE RUBBLE AND SAND.

THEY UNEARTHED BROKEN BASKETS AND BRONZE ARROWS.

THEY FOUND THOUSANDS OF COINS.

THEY UNCOVERED BEAUTIFUL MOSAICS AND RAGGED CLOTHING.

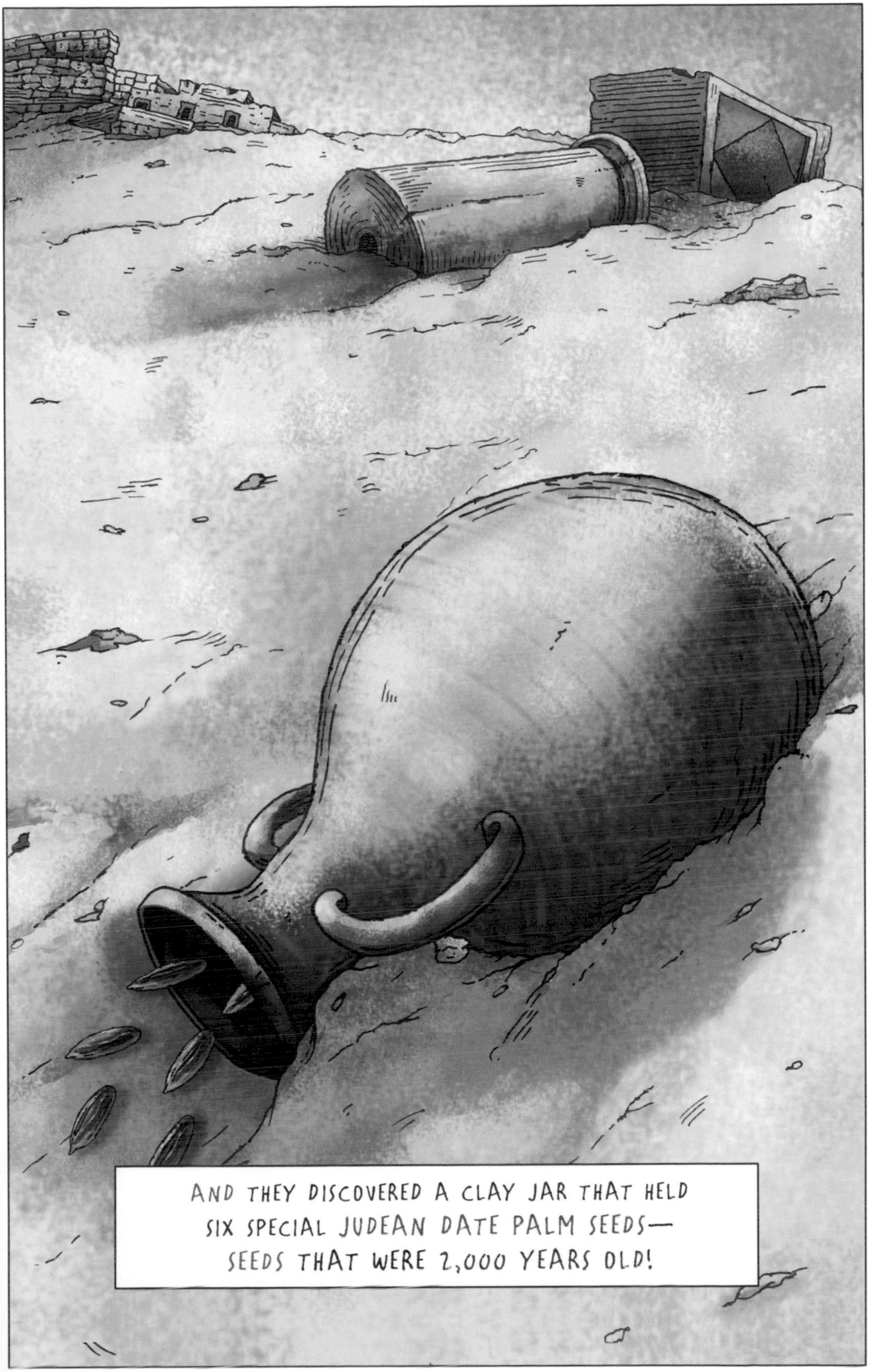
AND THEY DISCOVERED A CLAY JAR THAT HELD SIX SPECIAL JUDEAN DATE PALM SEEDS— SEEDS THAT WERE 2,000 YEARS OLD!

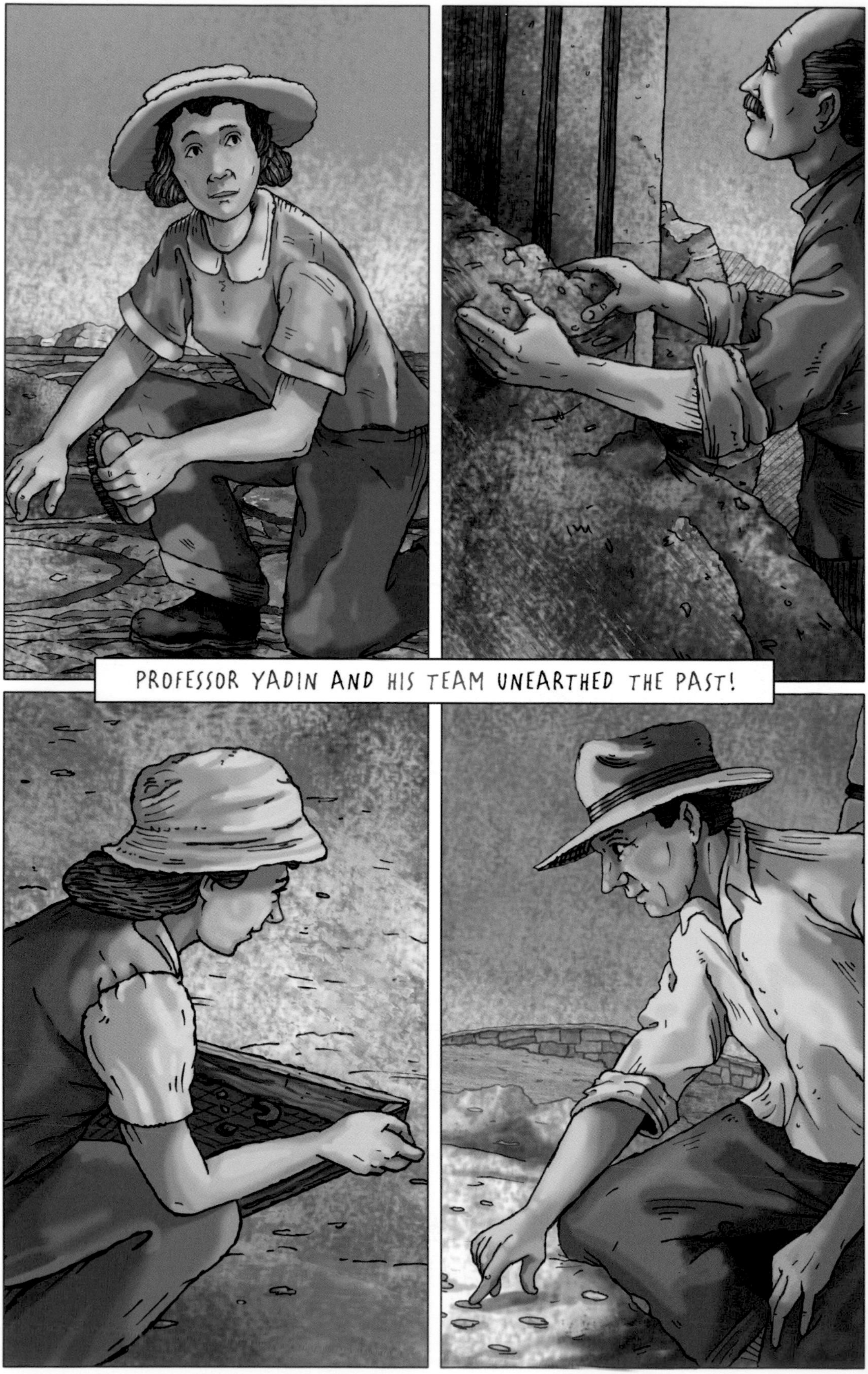
PROFESSOR YADIN AND HIS TEAM UNEARTHED THE PAST!

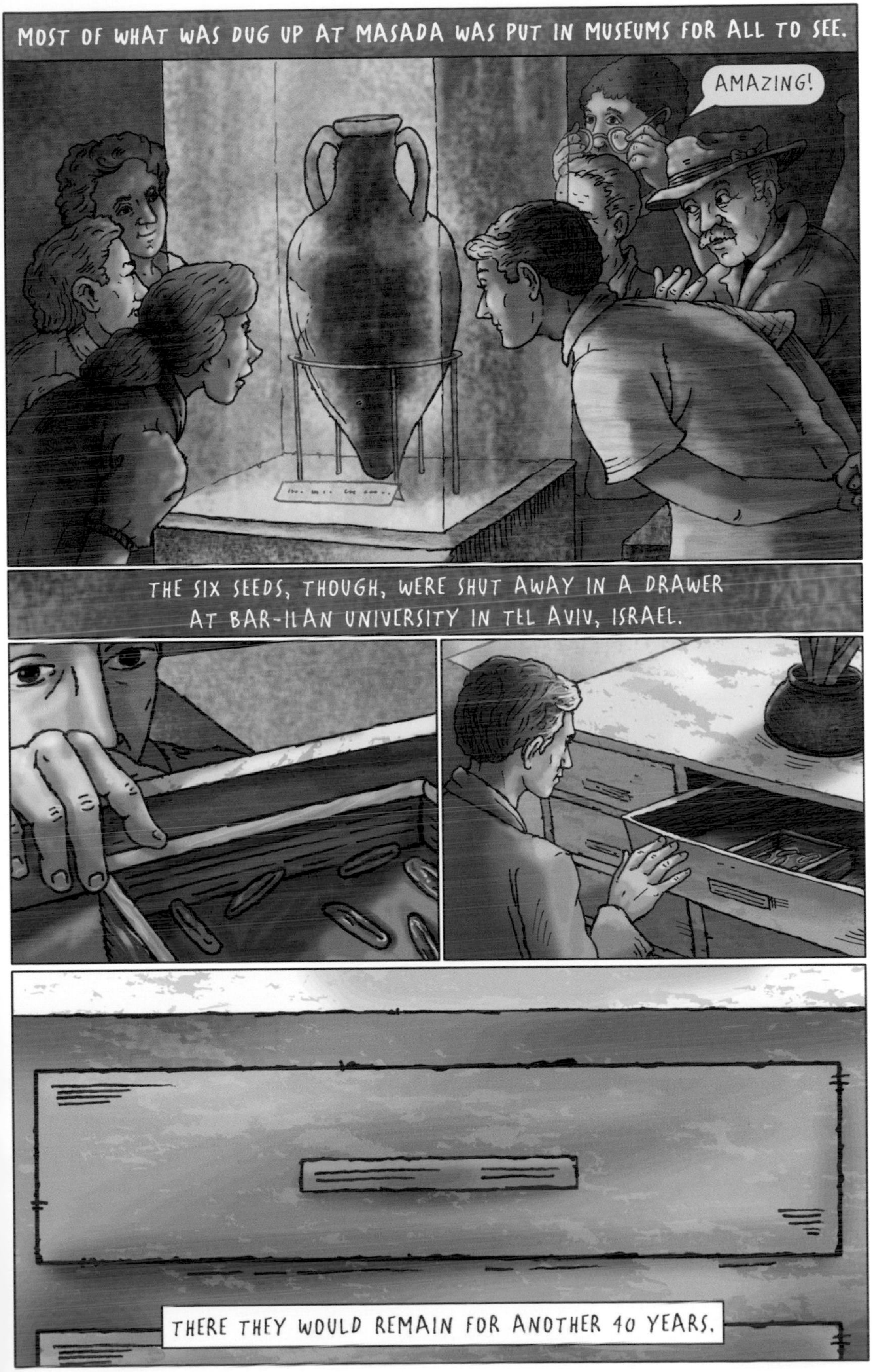
MOST OF WHAT WAS DUG UP AT MASADA WAS PUT IN MUSEUMS FOR ALL TO SEE.
AMAZING!
THE SIX SEEDS, THOUGH, WERE SHUT AWAY IN A DRAWER AT BAR-ILAN UNIVERSITY IN TEL AVIV, ISRAEL.
THERE THEY WOULD REMAIN FOR ANOTHER 40 YEARS.

IN 2004, EVERYTHING CHANGED.
SARAH SALLON, A DOCTOR SPECIALIZING IN CHILDREN'S DIGESTIVE DISEASES, READ ABOUT A 1,500-YEAR-OLD LOTUS SEED THAT SPROUTED.
SHE HAD A GREAT IDEA.

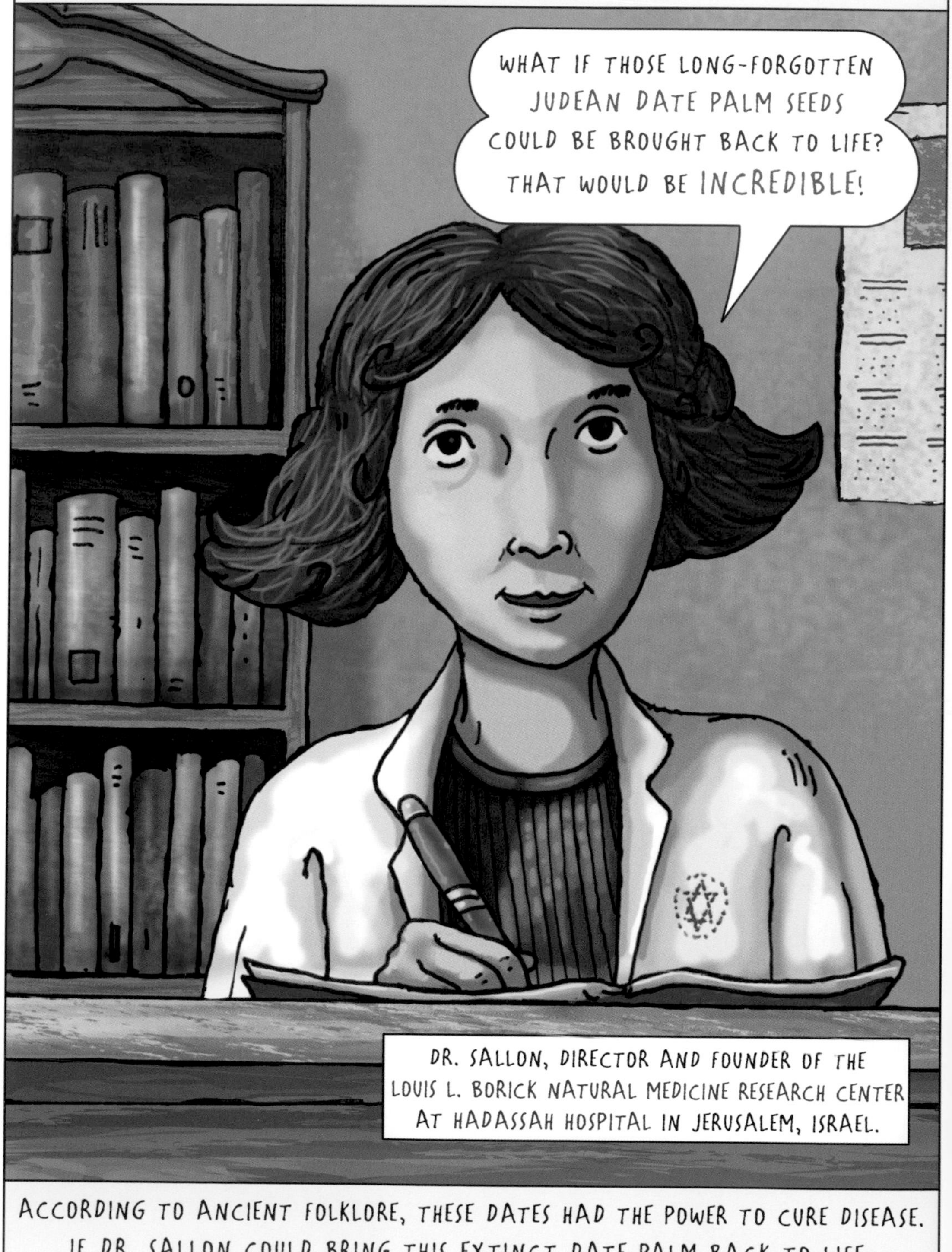

ACCORDING TO ANCIENT FOLKLORE, THESE DATES HAD THE POWER TO CURE DISEASE.
IF DR. SALLON COULD BRING THIS EXTINCT DATE PALM BACK TO LIFE, SHE COULD STUDY ITS HEALTH BENEFITS.

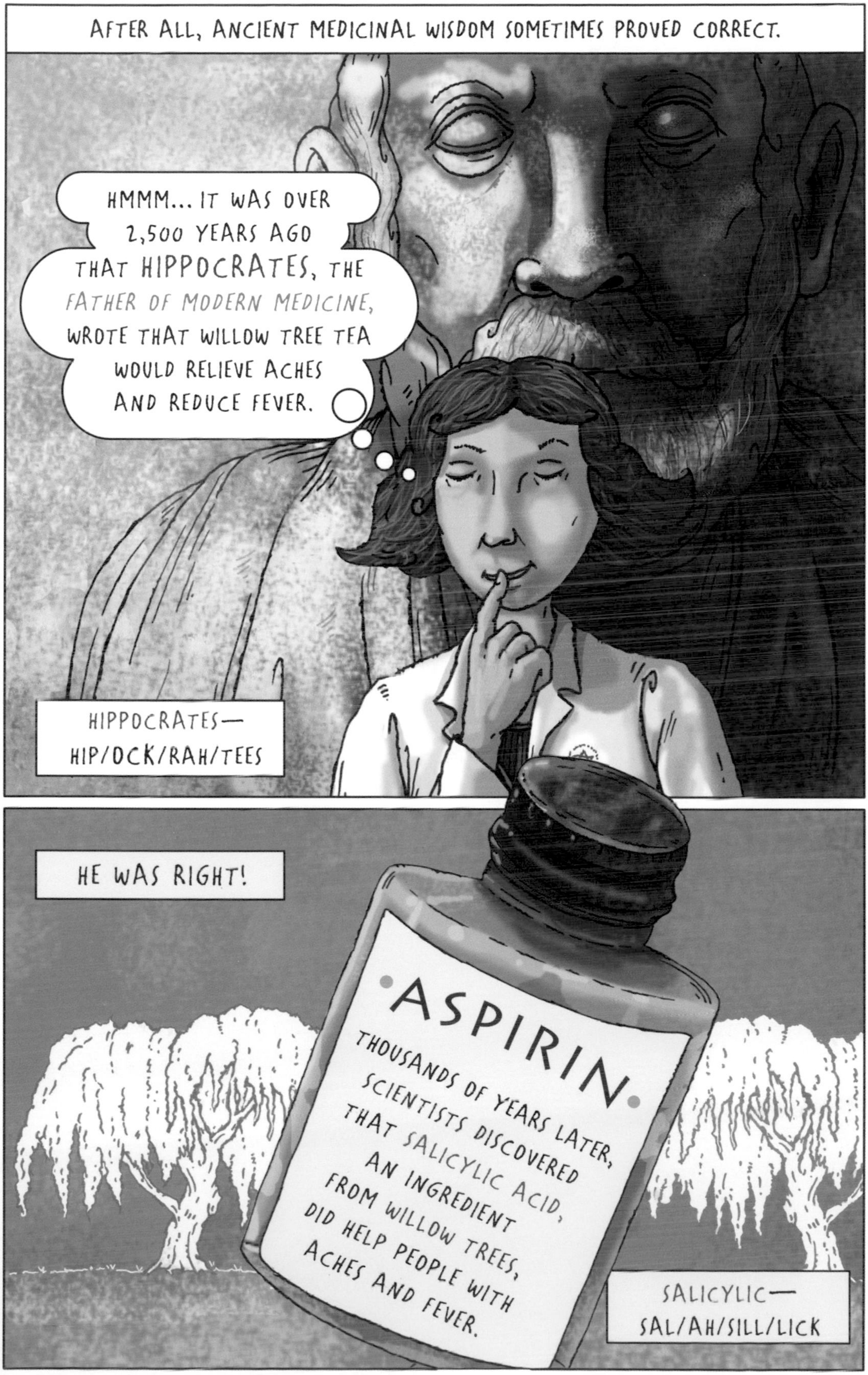
AFTER ALL, ANCIENT MEDICINAL WISDOM SOMETIMES PROVED CORRECT.
HMMM... IT WAS OVER 2,500 YEARS AGO THAT HIPPOCRATES, THE FATHER OF MODERN MEDICINE, WROTE THAT WILLOW TREE TEA WOULD RELIEVE ACHES AND REDUCE FEVER.
HIPPOCRATES— HIP/OCK/RAH/TEES
HE WAS RIGHT!
ASPIRIN
THOUSANDS OF YEARS LATER, SCIENTISTS DISCOVERED THAT SALICYLIC ACID, AN INGREDIENT FROM WILLOW TREES, DID HELP PEOPLE WITH ACHES AND FEVER.
SALICYLIC— SAL/AH/SILL/LICK

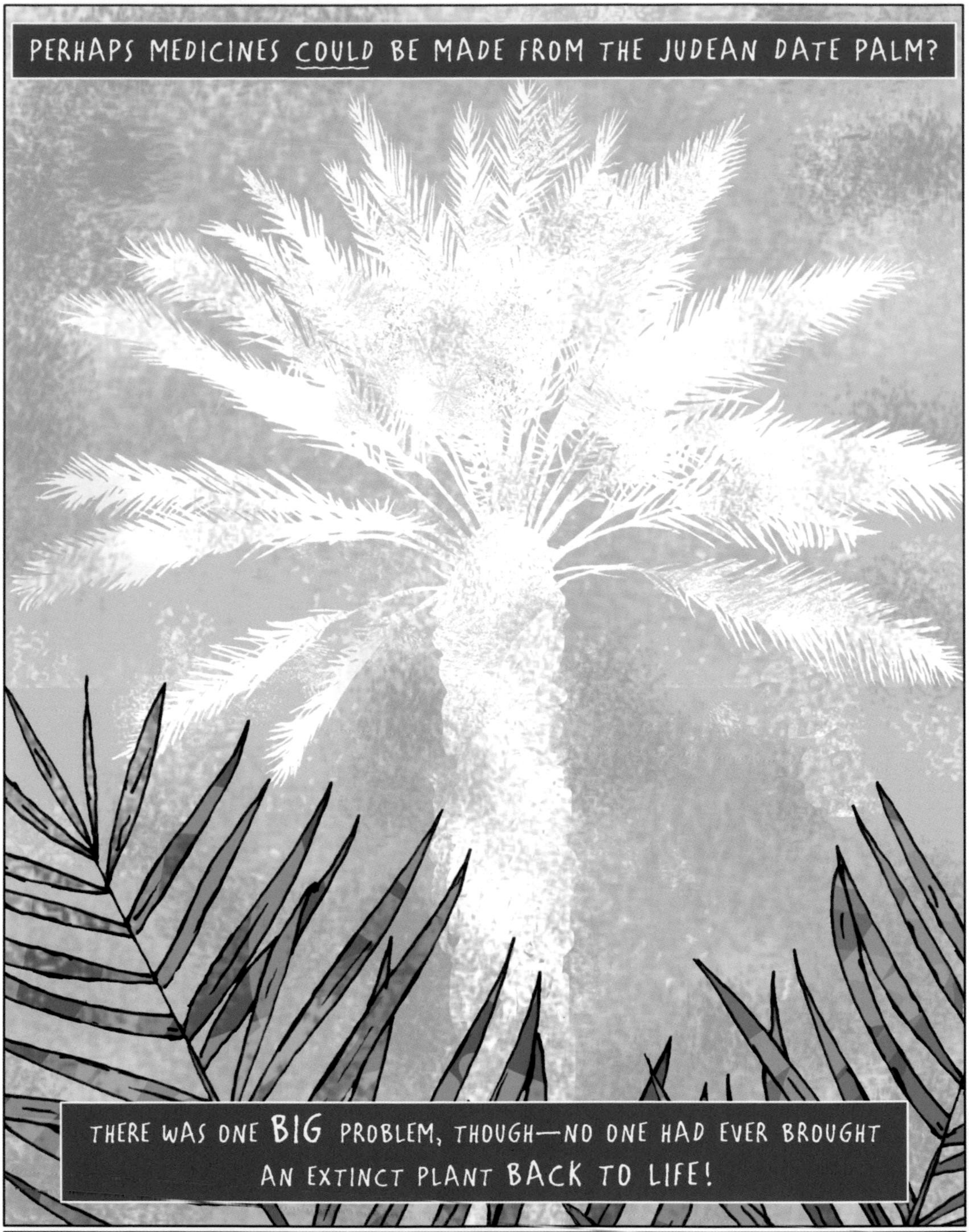
PERHAPS MEDICINES COULD BE MADE FROM THE JUDEAN DATE PALM?
THERE WAS ONE BIG PROBLEM, THOUGH—NO ONE HAD EVER BROUGHT AN EXTINCT PLANT BACK TO LIFE!

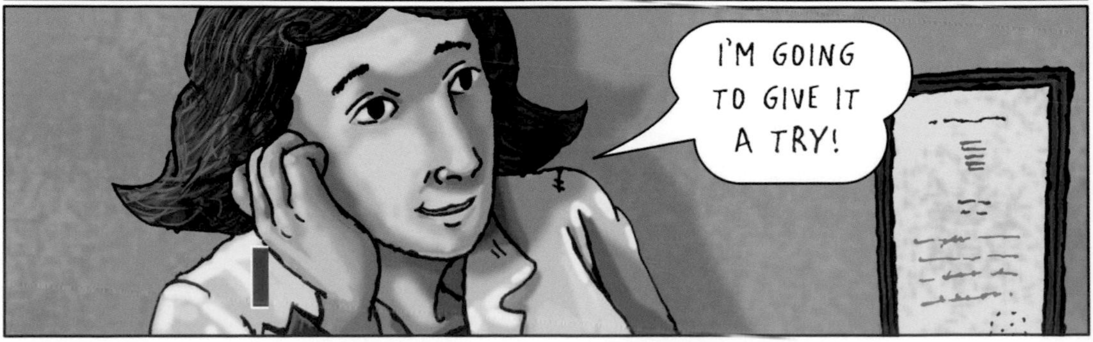
I'M GOING TO GIVE IT A TRY!

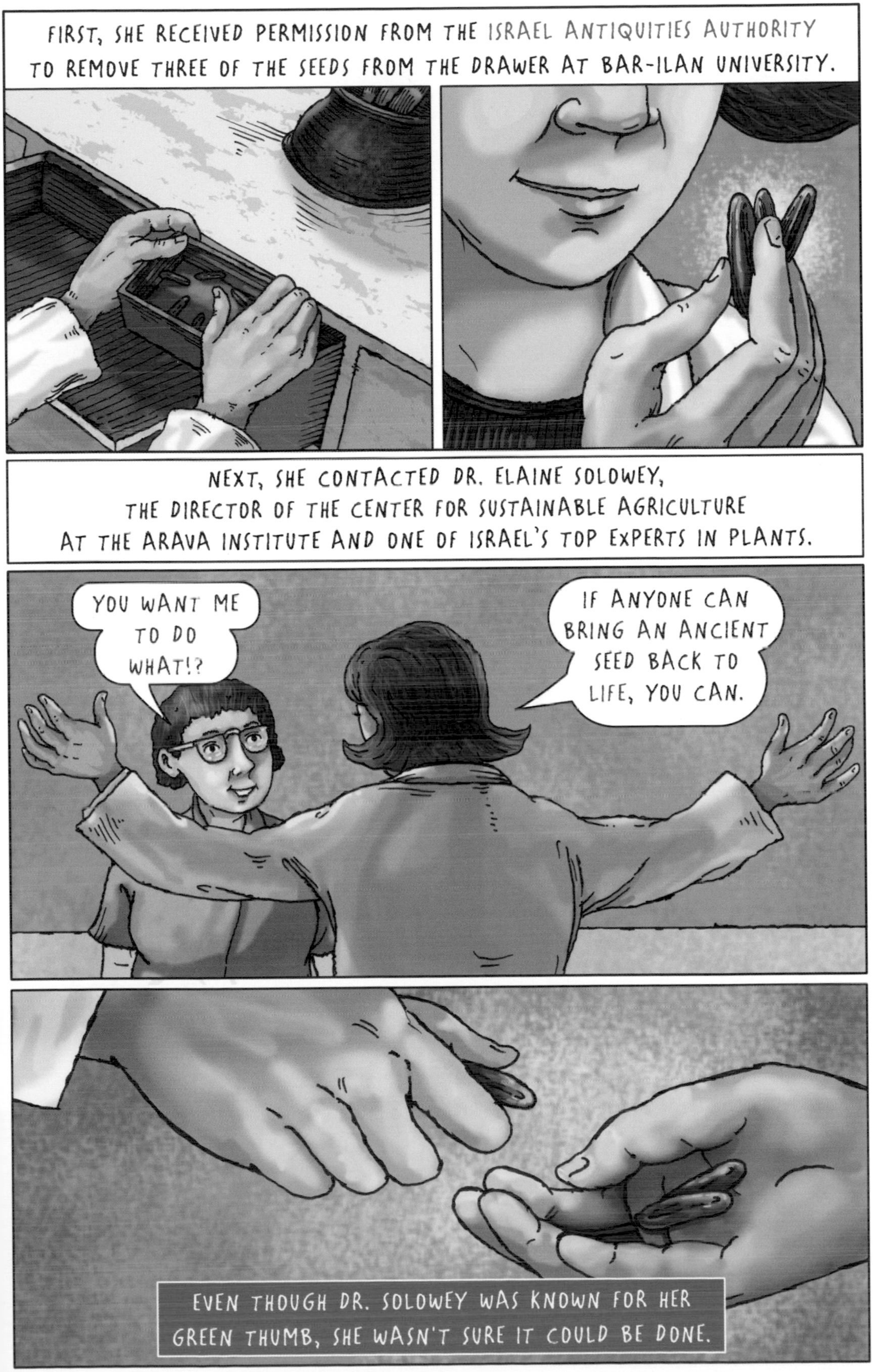
FIRST, SHE RECEIVED PERMISSION FROM THE ISRAEL ANTIQUITIES AUTHORITY TO REMOVE THREE OF THE SEEDS FROM THE DRAWER AT BAR-ILAN UNIVERSITY.
NEXT, SHE CONTACTED DR. ELAINE SOLOWEY, THE DIRECTOR OF THE CENTER FOR SUSTAINABLE AGRICULTURE AT THE ARAVA INSTITUTE AND ONE OF ISRAEL'S TOP EXPERTS IN PLANTS.
YOU WANT ME TO DO WHAT!?
IF ANYONE CAN BRING AN ANCIENT SEED BACK TO LIFE, YOU CAN.
EVEN THOUGH DR. SOLOWEY WAS KNOWN FOR HER GREEN THUMB, SHE WASN'T SURE IT COULD BE DONE.

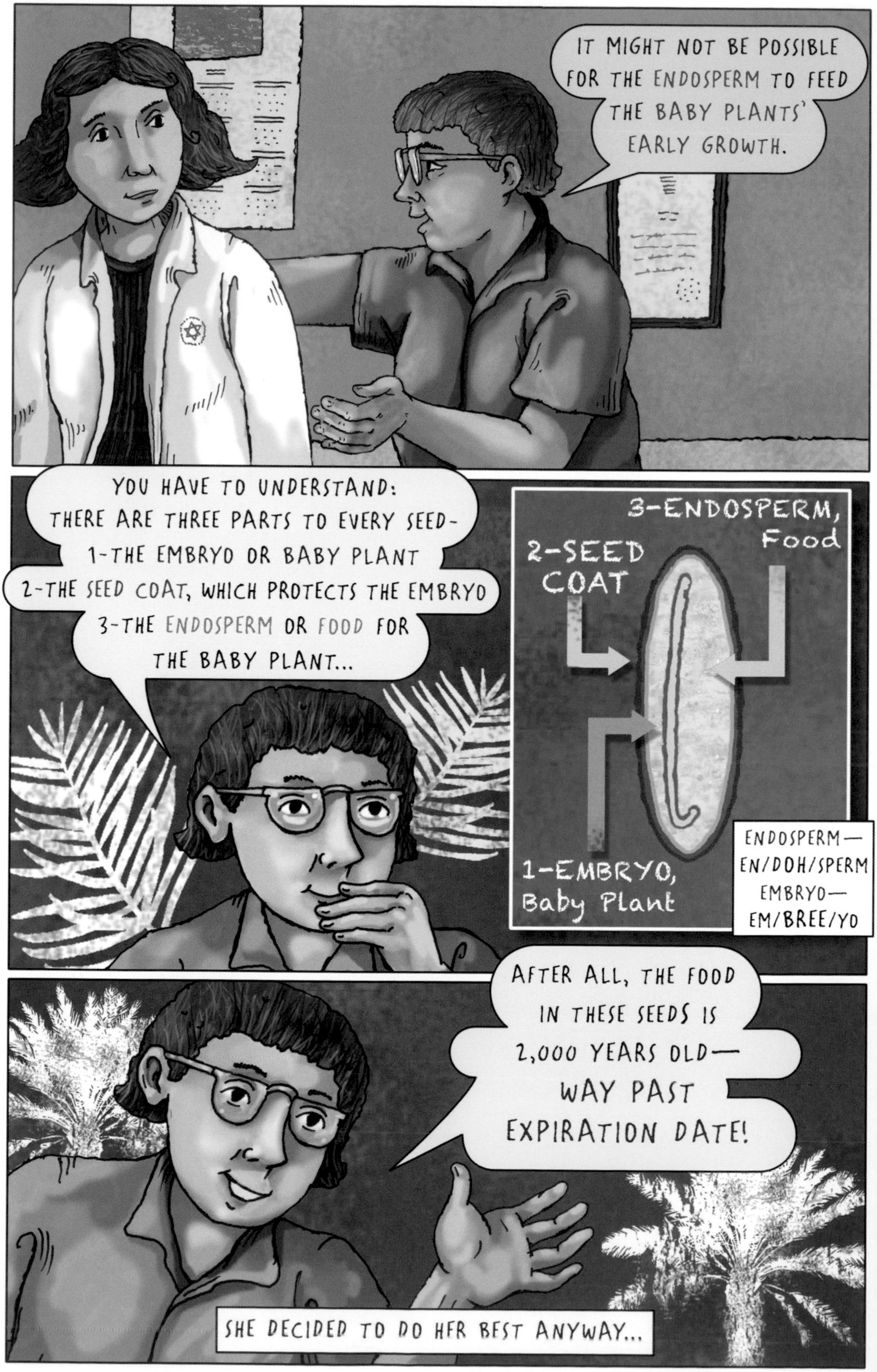
IT MIGHT NOT BE POSSIBLE FOR THE ENDOSPERM TO FEED THE BABY PLANTS' EARLY GROWTH.
YOU HAVE TO UNDERSTAND: THERE ARE THREE PARTS TO EVERY SEED- 1-THE EMBRYO OR BABY PLANT 2-THE SEED COAT, WHICH PROTECTS THE EMBRYO 3-THE ENDOSPERM OR FOOD FOR THE BABY PLANT...
3-ENDOSPERM, Food
2-SEED COAT
1-EMBRYO, Baby Plant
ENDOSPERM—EN/DOH/SPERM
EMBRYO—EM/BREE/YO
AFTER ALL, THE FOOD IN THESE SEEDS IS 2,000 YEARS OLD—WAY PAST EXPIRATION DATE!
SHE DECIDED TO DO HER BEST ANYWAY...

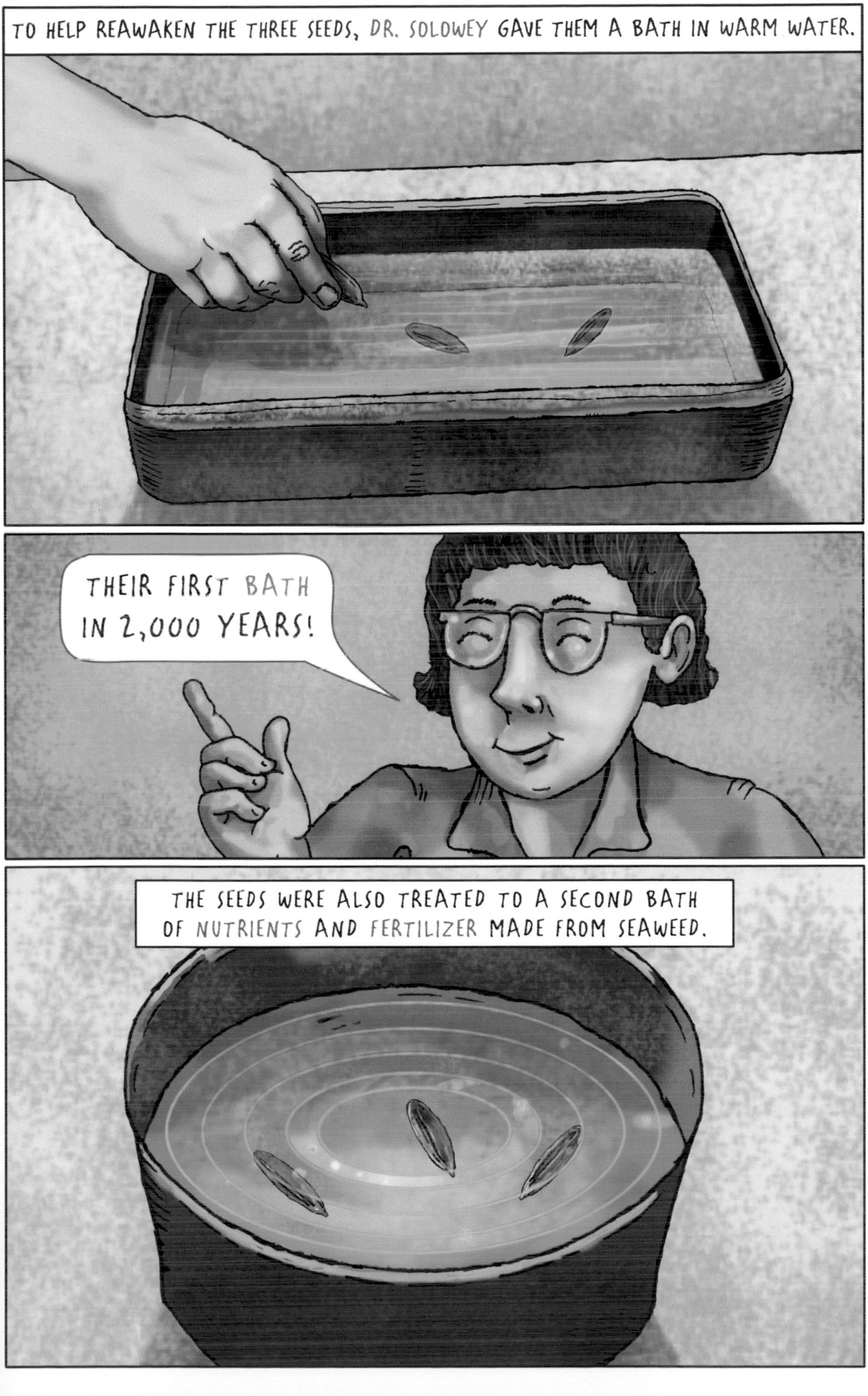
TO HELP REAWAKEN THE THREE SEEDS, DR. SOLOWEY GAVE THEM A BATH IN WARM WATER.
THEIR FIRST BATH IN 2,000 YEARS!
THE SEEDS WERE ALSO TREATED TO A SECOND BATH OF NUTRIENTS AND FERTILIZER MADE FROM SEAWEED.

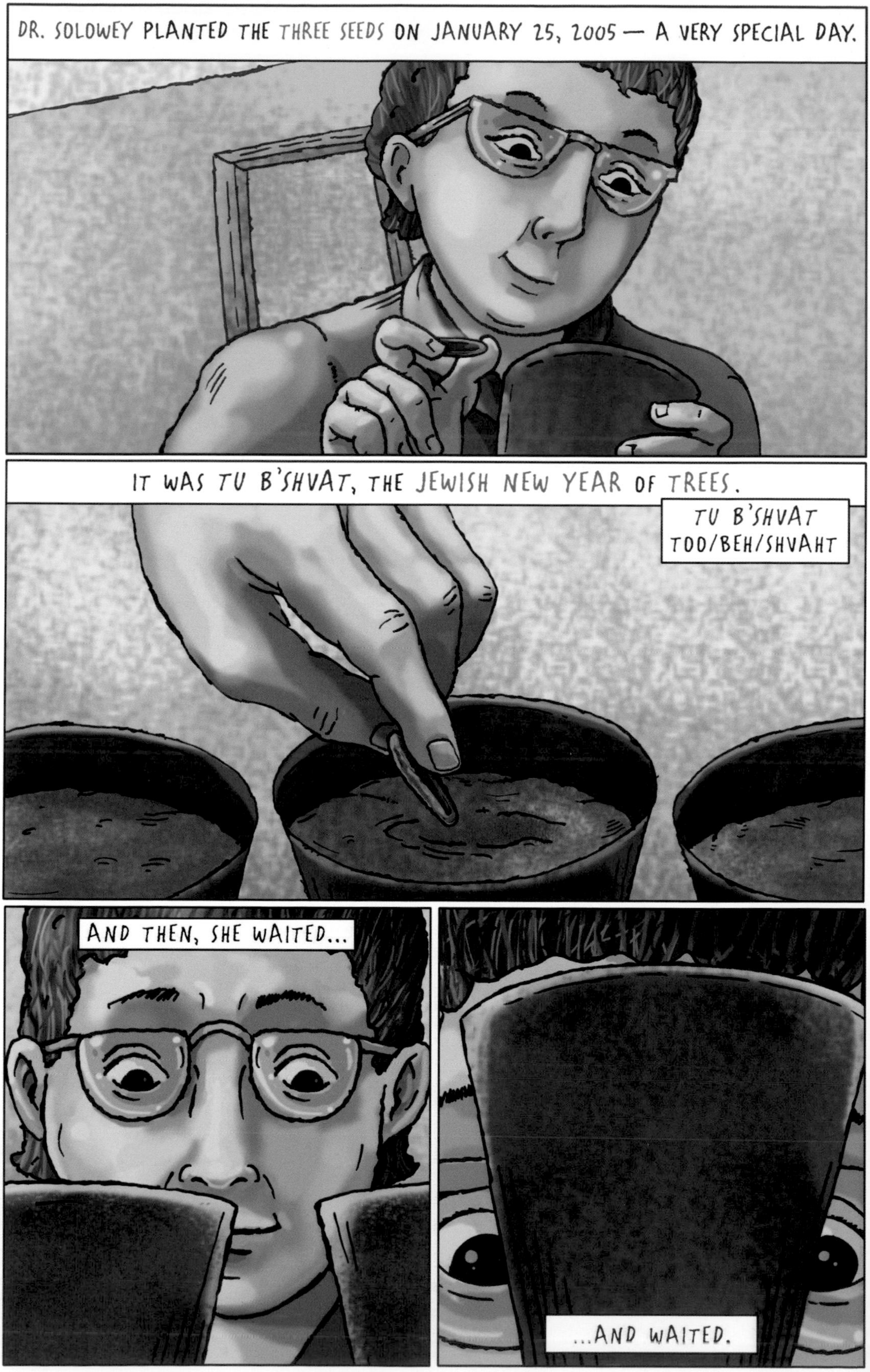
DR. SOLOWEY PLANTED THE THREE SEEDS ON JANUARY 25, 2005 — A VERY SPECIAL DAY.
IT WAS TU B'SHVAT, THE JEWISH NEW YEAR OF TREES.
TU B'SHVAT TOO/BEH/SHVAHT
AND THEN, SHE WAITED...
...AND WAITED.

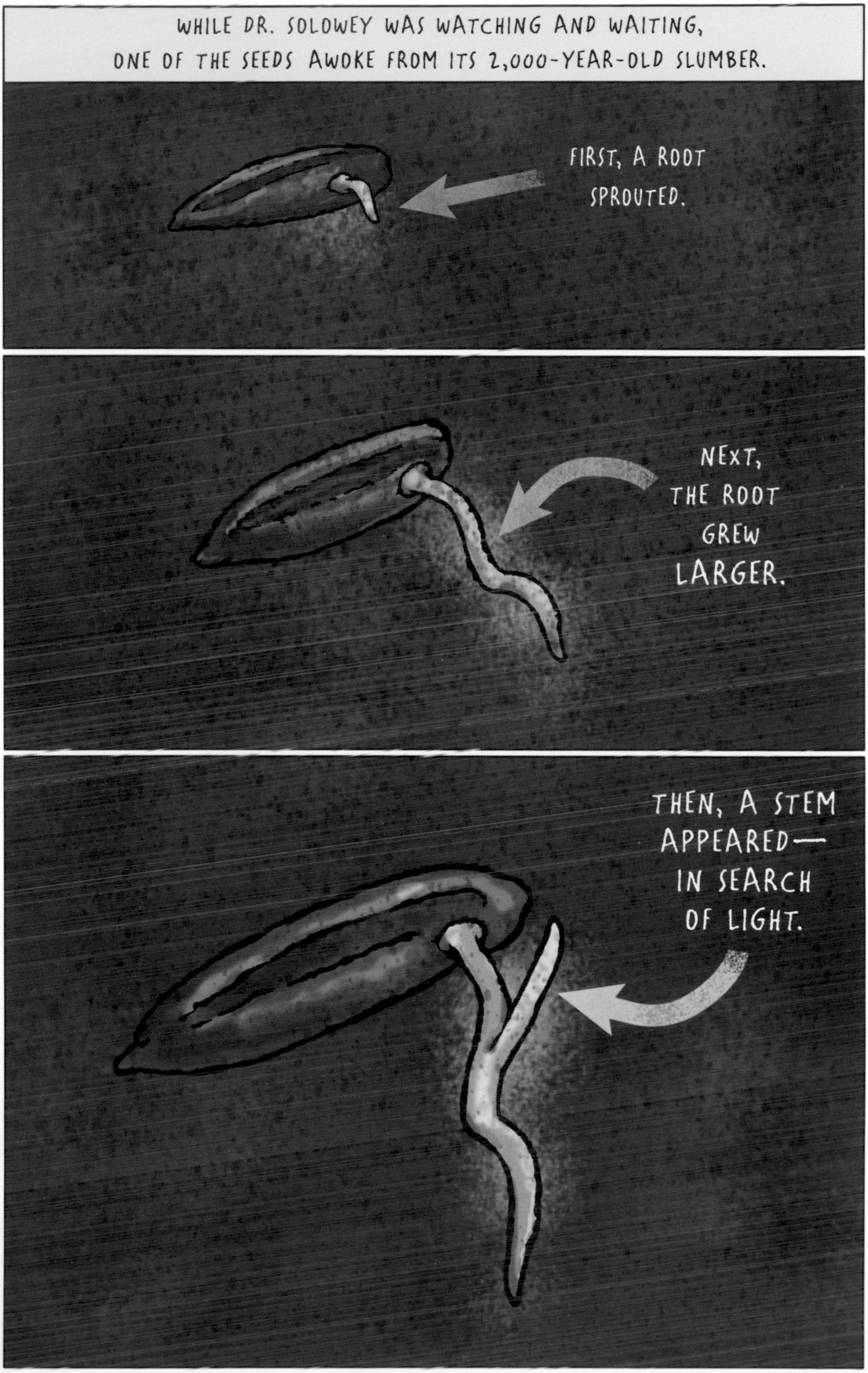
WHILE DR. SOLOWEY WAS WATCHING AND WAITING, ONE OF THE SEEDS AWOKE FROM ITS 2,000-YEAR-OLD SLUMBER.
FIRST, A ROOT SPROUTED.
NEXT, THE ROOT GREW LARGER.
THEN, A STEM APPEARED— IN SEARCH OF LIGHT.

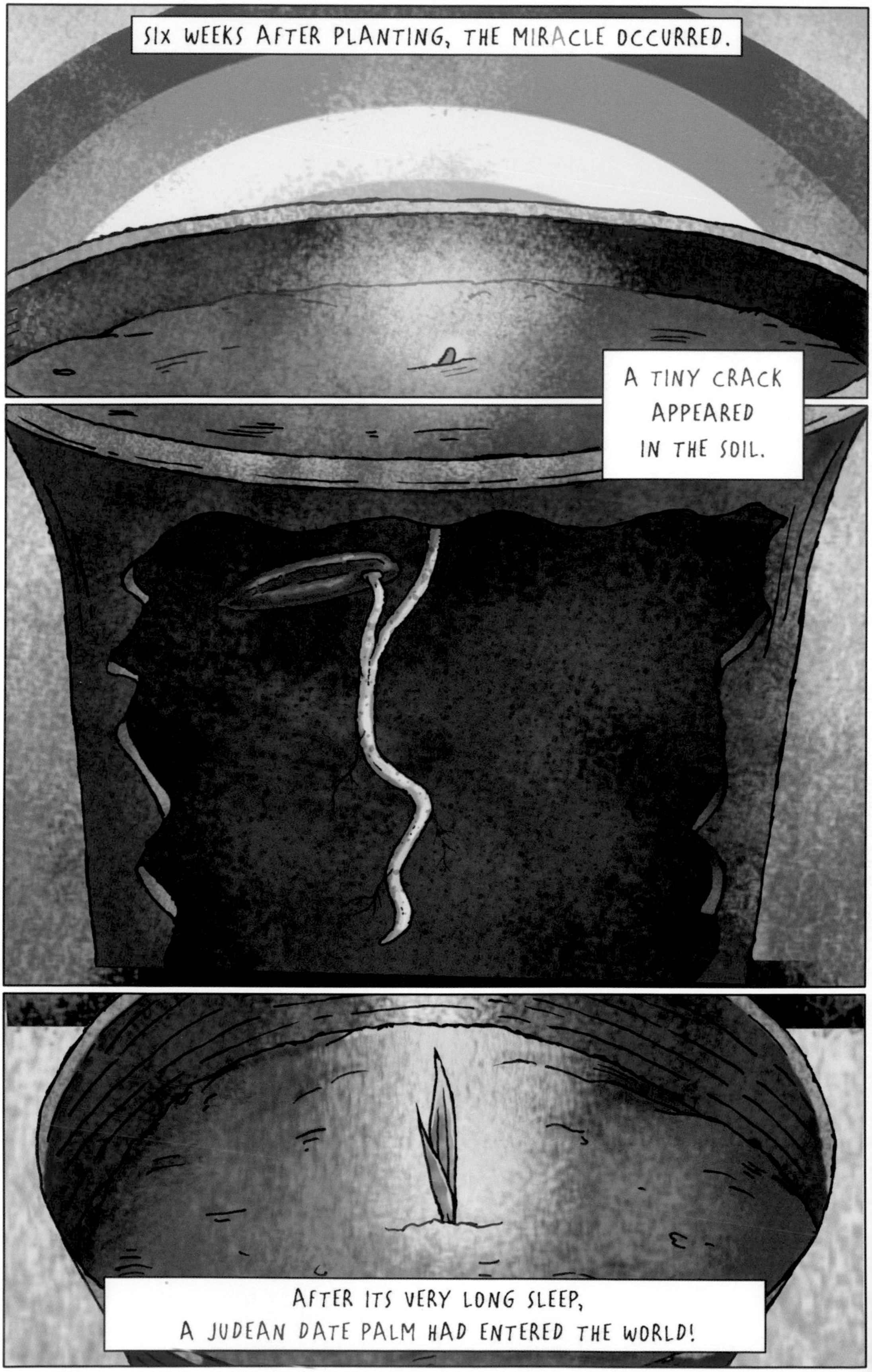
SIX WEEKS AFTER PLANTING, THE MIRACLE OCCURRED.
A TINY CRACK APPEARED IN THE SOIL.
AFTER ITS VERY LONG SLEEP, A JUDEAN DATE PALM HAD ENTERED THE WORLD!

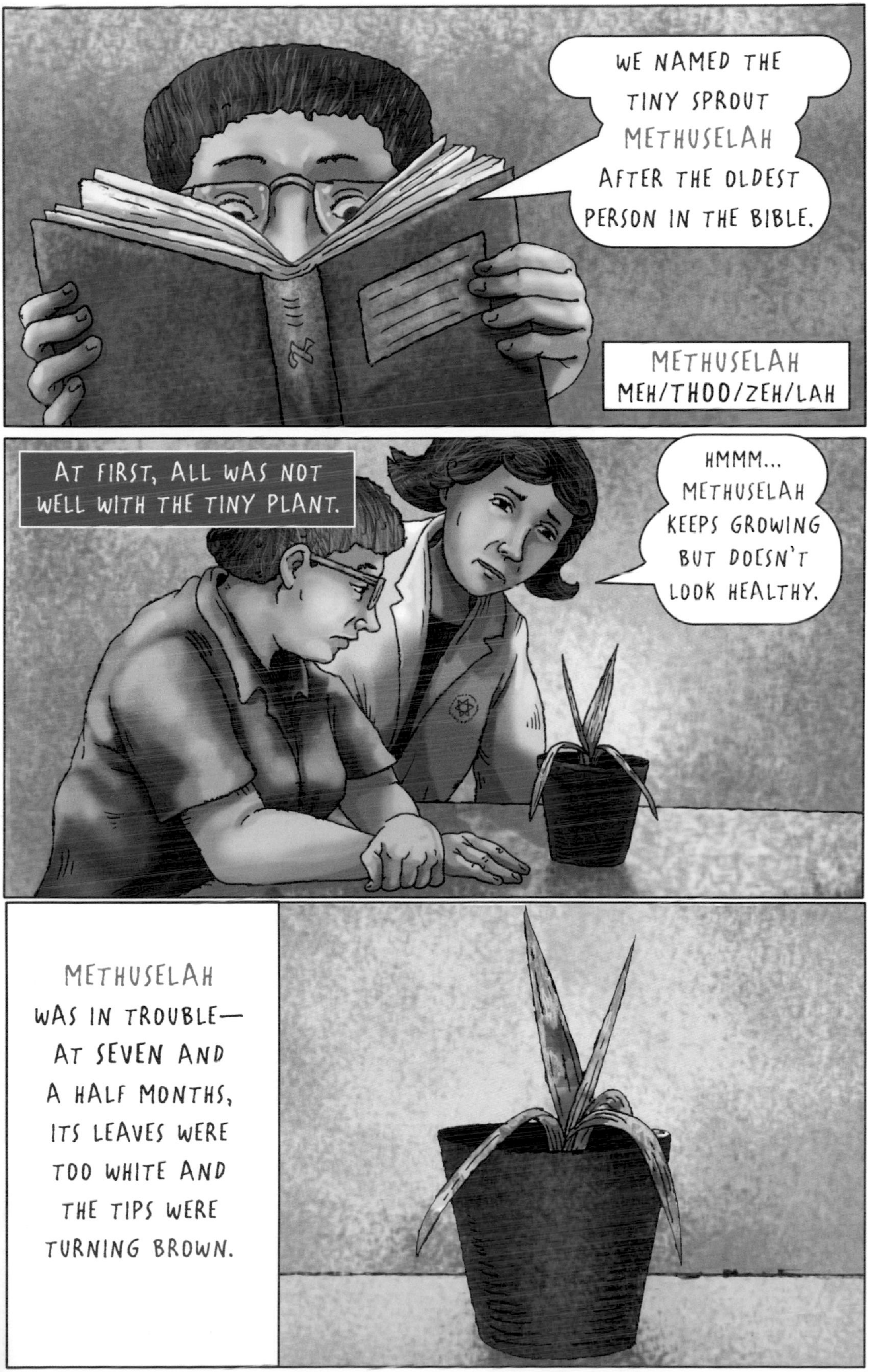
WE NAMED THE TINY SPROUT METHUSELAH AFTER THE OLDEST PERSON IN THE BIBLE.
METHUSELAH
MEH/THOO/ZEH/LAH
AT FIRST, ALL WAS NOT WELL WITH THE TINY PLANT.
HMMM... METHUSELAH KEEPS GROWING BUT DOESN'T LOOK HEALTHY.
METHUSELAH WAS IN TROUBLE— AT SEVEN AND A HALF MONTHS, ITS LEAVES WERE TOO WHITE AND THE TIPS WERE TURNING BROWN.

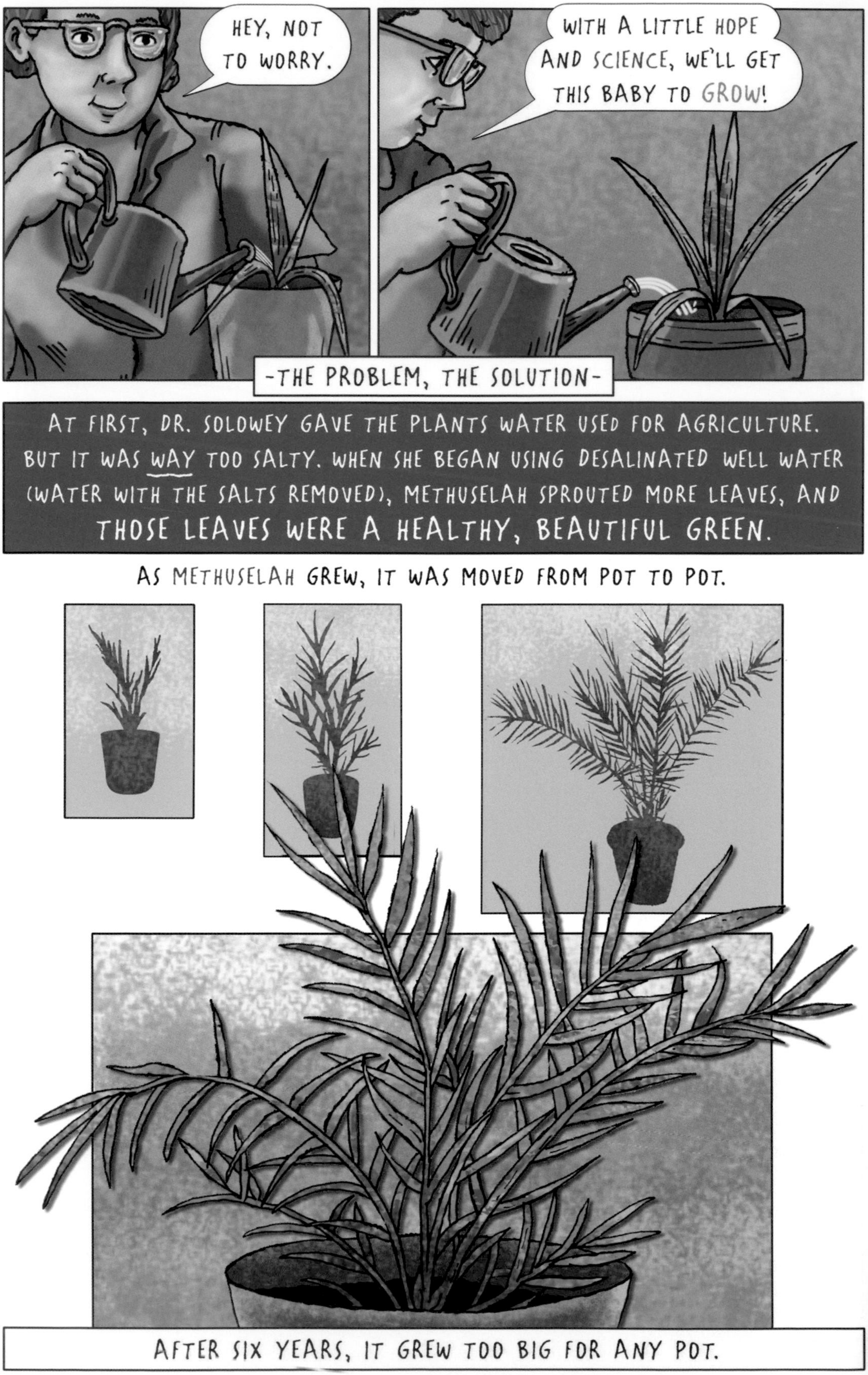
HEY, NOT TO WORRY.
WITH A LITTLE HOPE AND SCIENCE, WE'LL GET THIS BABY TO GROW!
-THE PROBLEM, THE SOLUTION-
AT FIRST, DR. SOLOWEY GAVE THE PLANTS WATER USED FOR AGRICULTURE. BUT IT WAS WAY TOO SALTY. WHEN SHE BEGAN USING DESALINATED WELL WATER (WATER WITH THE SALTS REMOVED), METHUSELAH SPROUTED MORE LEAVES, AND THOSE LEAVES WERE A HEALTHY, BEAUTIFUL GREEN.
AS METHUSELAH GREW, IT WAS MOVED FROM POT TO POT.
AFTER SIX YEARS, IT GREW TOO BIG FOR ANY POT.

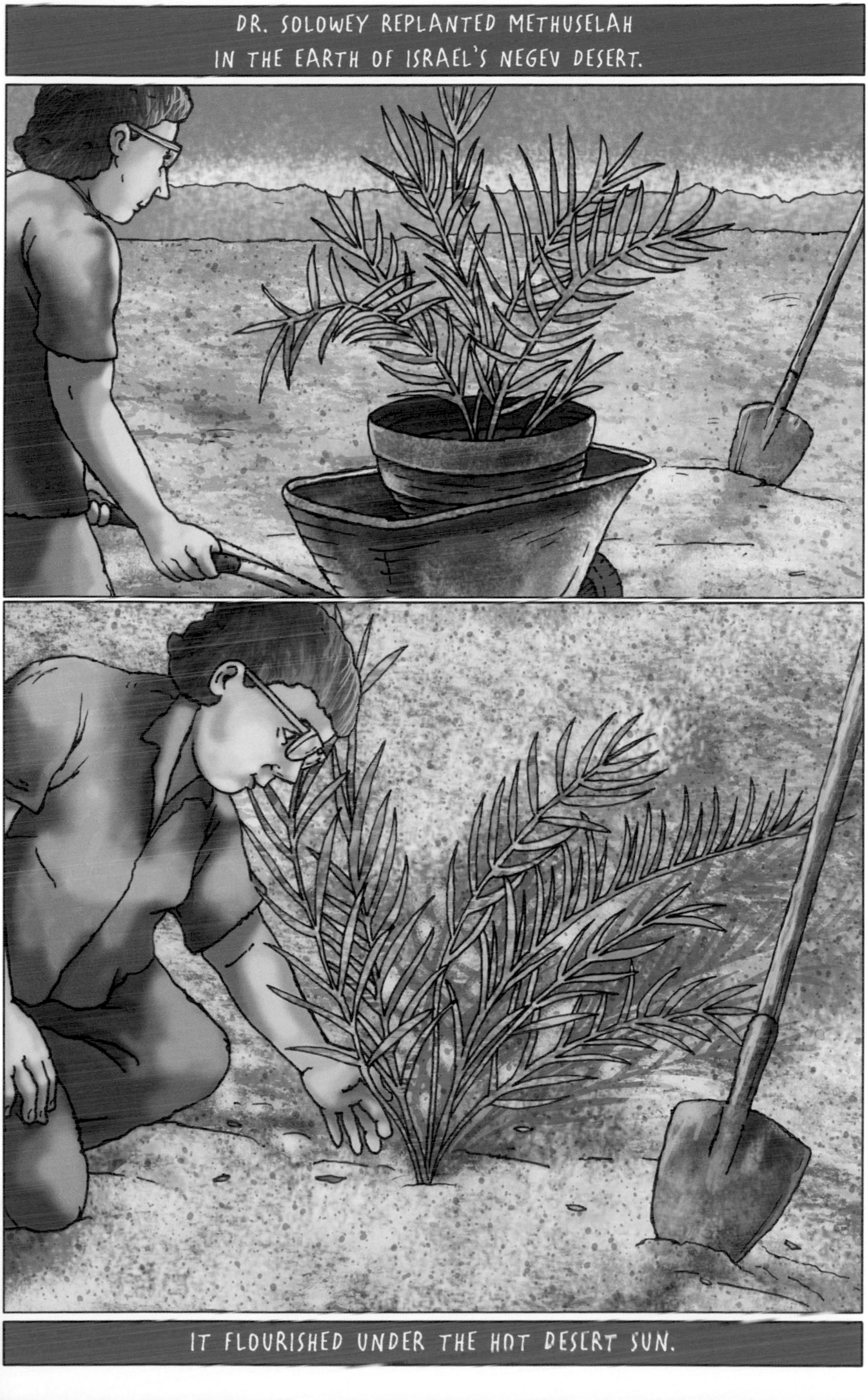
DR. SOLOWEY REPLANTED METHUSELAH IN THE EARTH OF ISRAEL'S NEGEV DESERT.
IT FLOURISHED UNDER THE HOT DESERT SUN.

POLLINATION

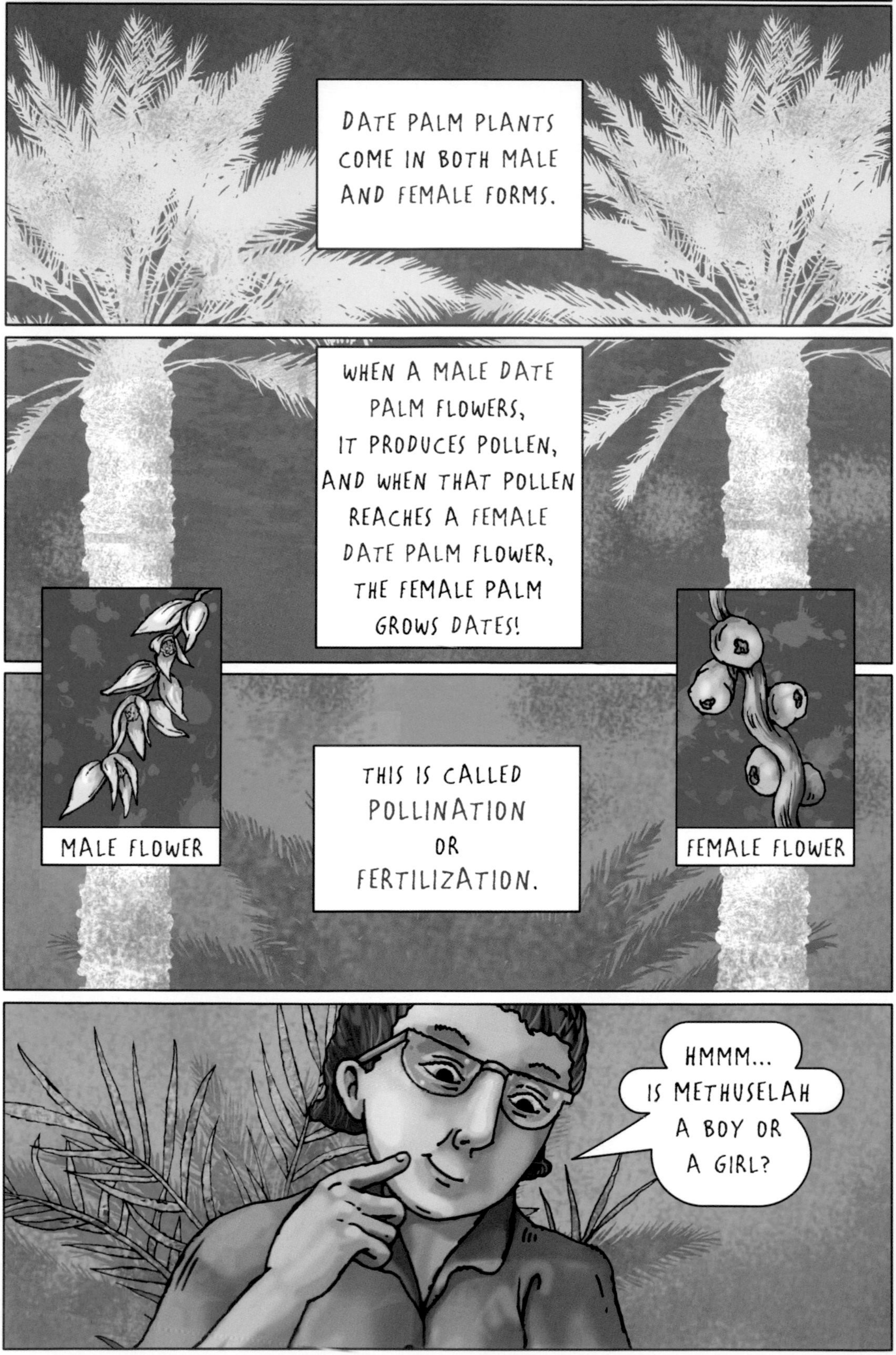
DATE PALM PLANTS COME IN BOTH MALE AND FEMALE FORMS.
WHEN A MALE DATE PALM FLOWERS, IT PRODUCES POLLEN, AND WHEN THAT POLLEN REACHES A FEMALE DATE PALM FLOWER, THE FEMALE PALM GROWS DATES!
MALE FLOWER
FEMALE FLOWER
THIS IS CALLED POLLINATION OR FERTILIZATION.
HMMM... IS METHUSELAH A BOY OR A GIRL?

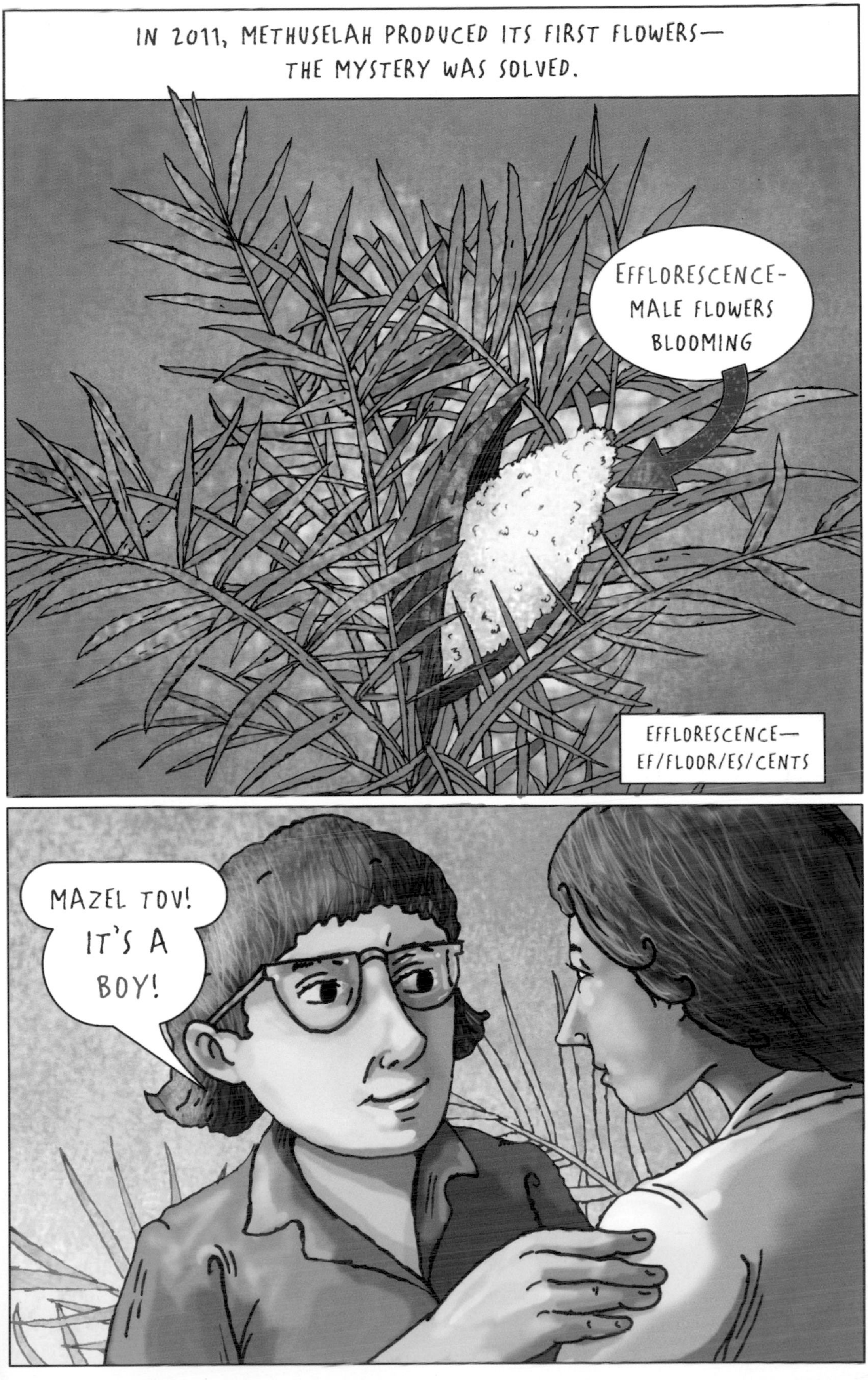
IN 2011, METHUSELAH PRODUCED ITS FIRST FLOWERS—
THE MYSTERY WAS SOLVED.
EFFLORESCENCE-
MALE FLOWERS
BLOOMING
EFFLORESCENCE—
EF/FLOOR/ES/CENTS
MAZEL TOV!
IT'S A
BOY!

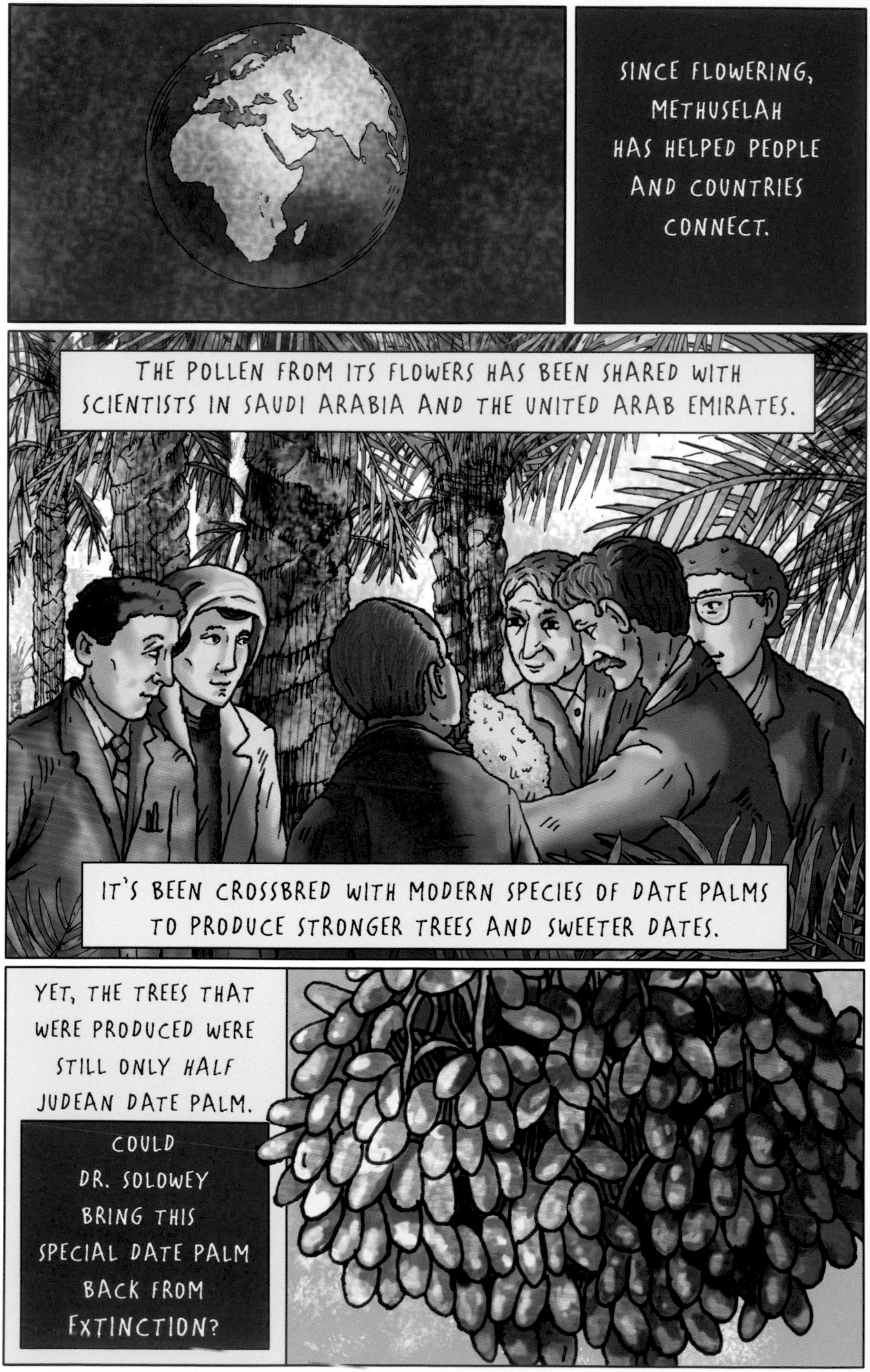
SINCE FLOWERING, METHUSELAH HAS HELPED PEOPLE AND COUNTRIES CONNECT.
THE POLLEN FROM ITS FLOWERS HAS BEEN SHARED WITH SCIENTISTS IN SAUDI ARABIA AND THE UNITED ARAB EMIRATES.
IT'S BEEN CROSSBRED WITH MODERN SPECIES OF DATE PALMS TO PRODUCE STRONGER TREES AND SWEETER DATES.
YET, THE TREES THAT WERE PRODUCED WERE STILL ONLY *HALF* JUDEAN DATE PALM.
COULD DR. SOLOWEY BRING THIS SPECIAL DATE PALM BACK FROM EXTINCTION?

PART THREE

·REBIRTH·

MIRACLES DO NOT, IN FACT,
BREAK THE LAWS OF NATURE.

C. S. LEWIS

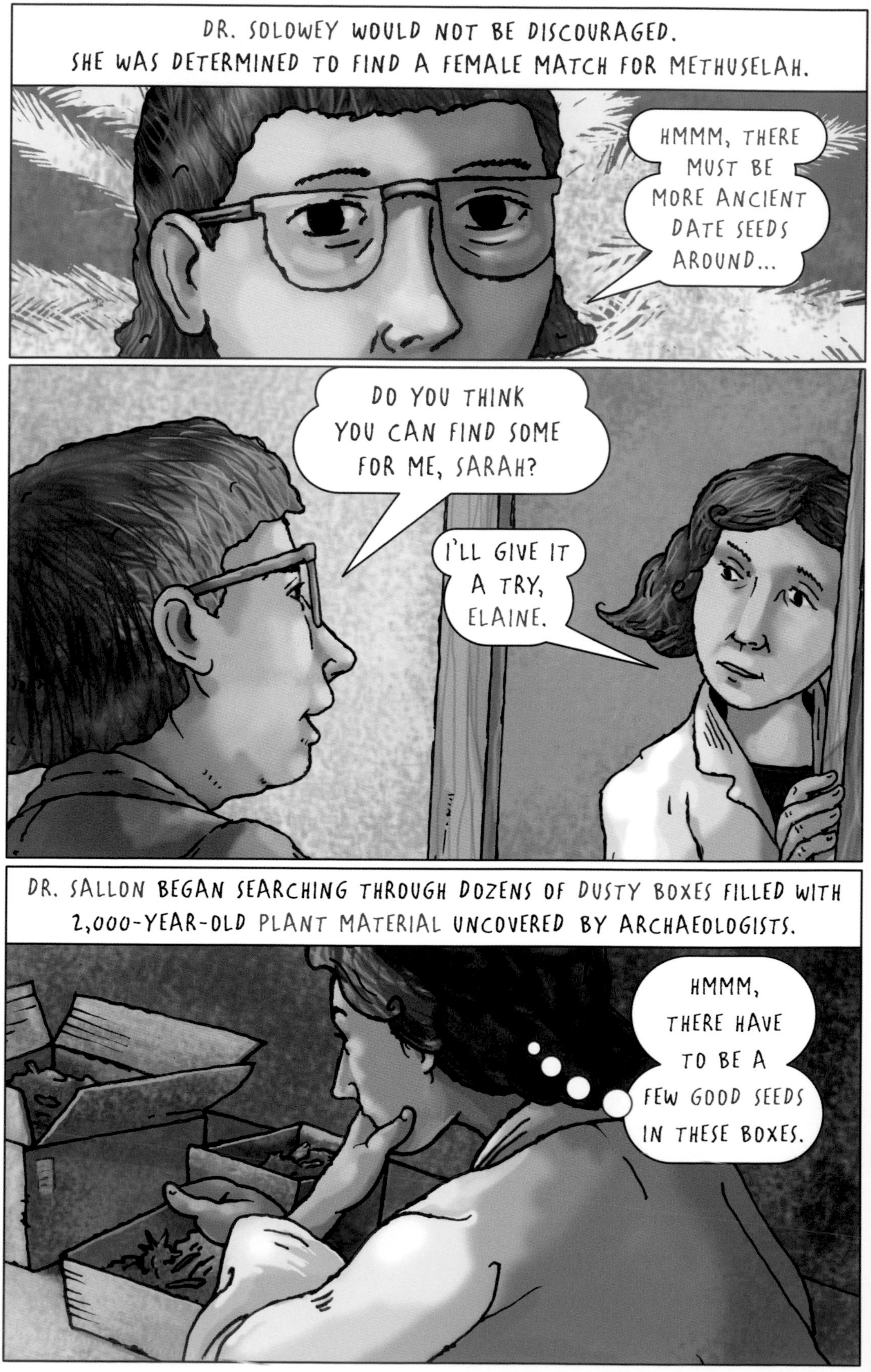
DR. SOLOWEY WOULD NOT BE DISCOURAGED. SHE WAS DETERMINED TO FIND A FEMALE MATCH FOR METHUSELAH.
HMMM, THERE MUST BE MORE ANCIENT DATE SEEDS AROUND...
DO YOU THINK YOU CAN FIND SOME FOR ME, SARAH?
I'LL GIVE IT A TRY, ELAINE.
DR. SALLON BEGAN SEARCHING THROUGH DOZENS OF DUSTY BOXES FILLED WITH 2,000-YEAR-OLD PLANT MATERIAL UNCOVERED BY ARCHAEOLOGISTS.
HMMM, THERE HAVE TO BE A FEW GOOD SEEDS IN THESE BOXES.

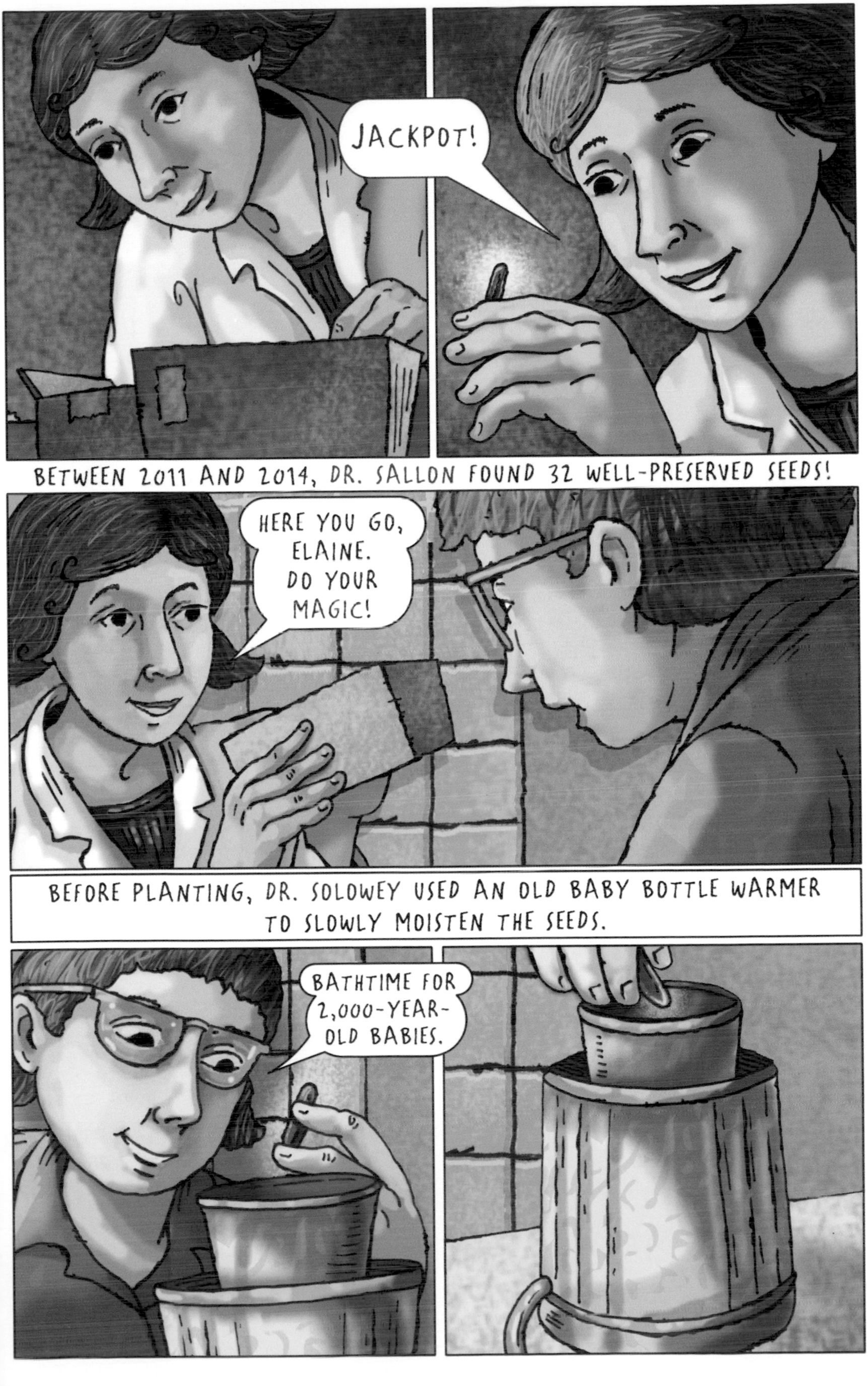
JACKPOT!
BETWEEN 2011 AND 2014, DR. SALLON FOUND 32 WELL-PRESERVED SEEDS!
HERE YOU GO, ELAINE. DO YOUR MAGIC!
BEFORE PLANTING, DR. SOLOWEY USED AN OLD BABY BOTTLE WARMER TO SLOWLY MOISTEN THE SEEDS.
BATHTIME FOR 2,000-YEAR-OLD BABIES.

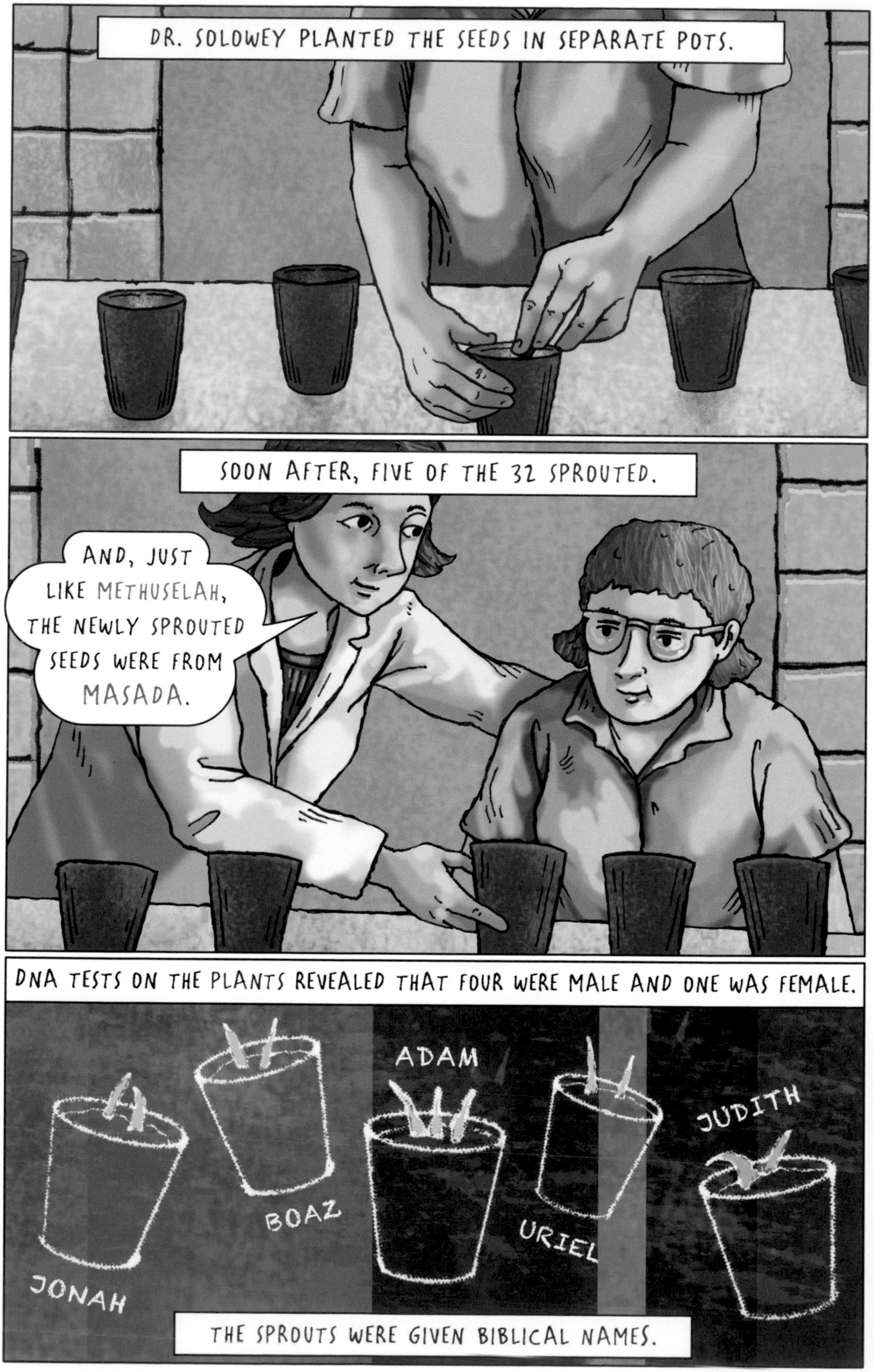
DR. SOLOWEY PLANTED THE SEEDS IN SEPARATE POTS.
SOON AFTER, FIVE OF THE 32 SPROUTED.
AND, JUST LIKE METHUSELAH, THE NEWLY SPROUTED SEEDS WERE FROM MASADA.
DNA TESTS ON THE PLANTS REVEALED THAT FOUR WERE MALE AND ONE WAS FEMALE.
ADAM
JUDITH
BOAZ
URIEL
JONAH
THE SPROUTS WERE GIVEN BIBLICAL NAMES.

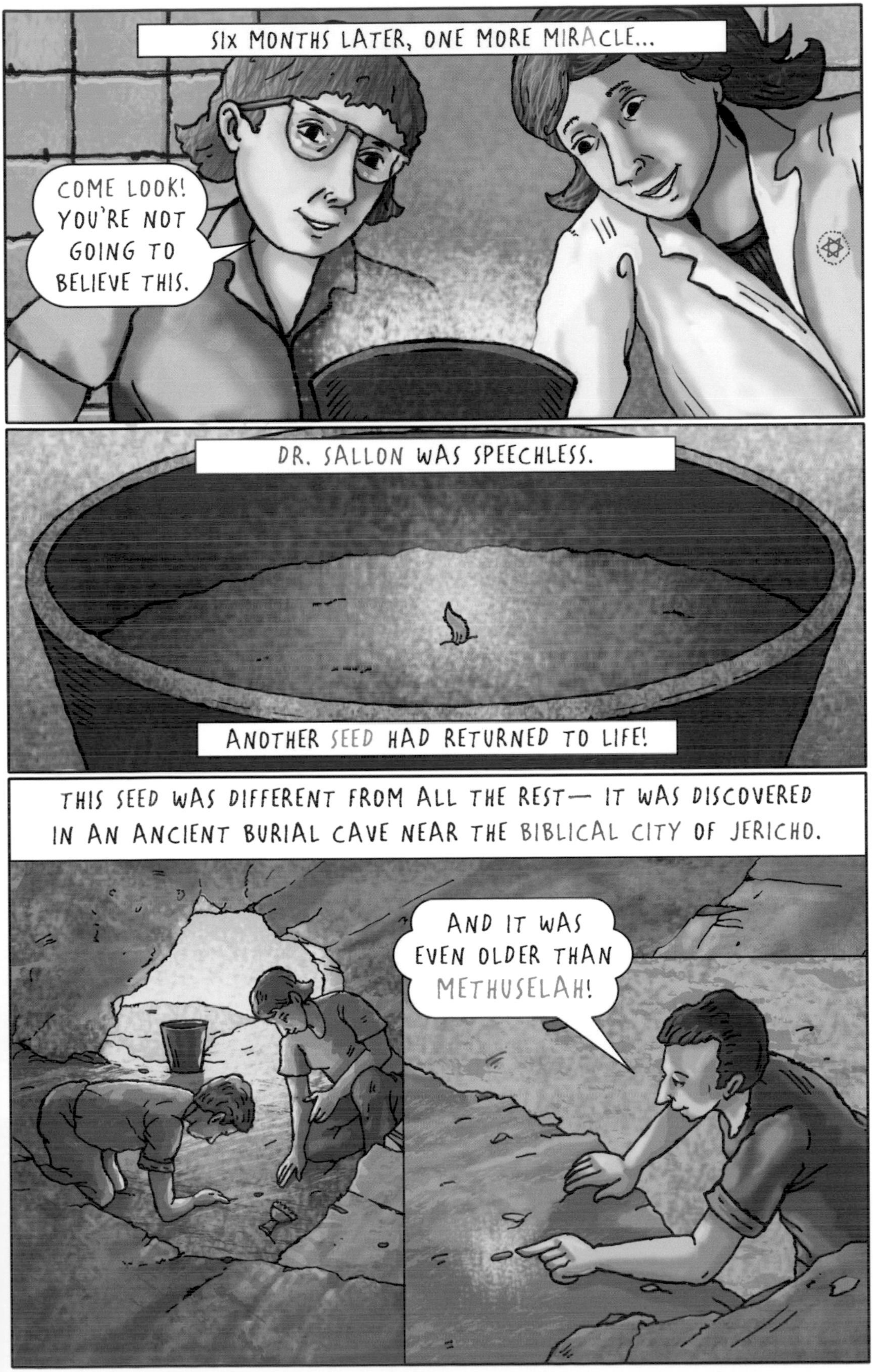
SIX MONTHS LATER, ONE MORE MIRACLE...
COME LOOK! YOU'RE NOT GOING TO BELIEVE THIS.
DR. SALLON WAS SPEECHLESS.
ANOTHER SEED HAD RETURNED TO LIFE!
THIS SEED WAS DIFFERENT FROM ALL THE REST— IT WAS DISCOVERED IN AN ANCIENT BURIAL CAVE NEAR THE BIBLICAL CITY OF JERICHO.
AND IT WAS EVEN OLDER THAN METHUSELAH!

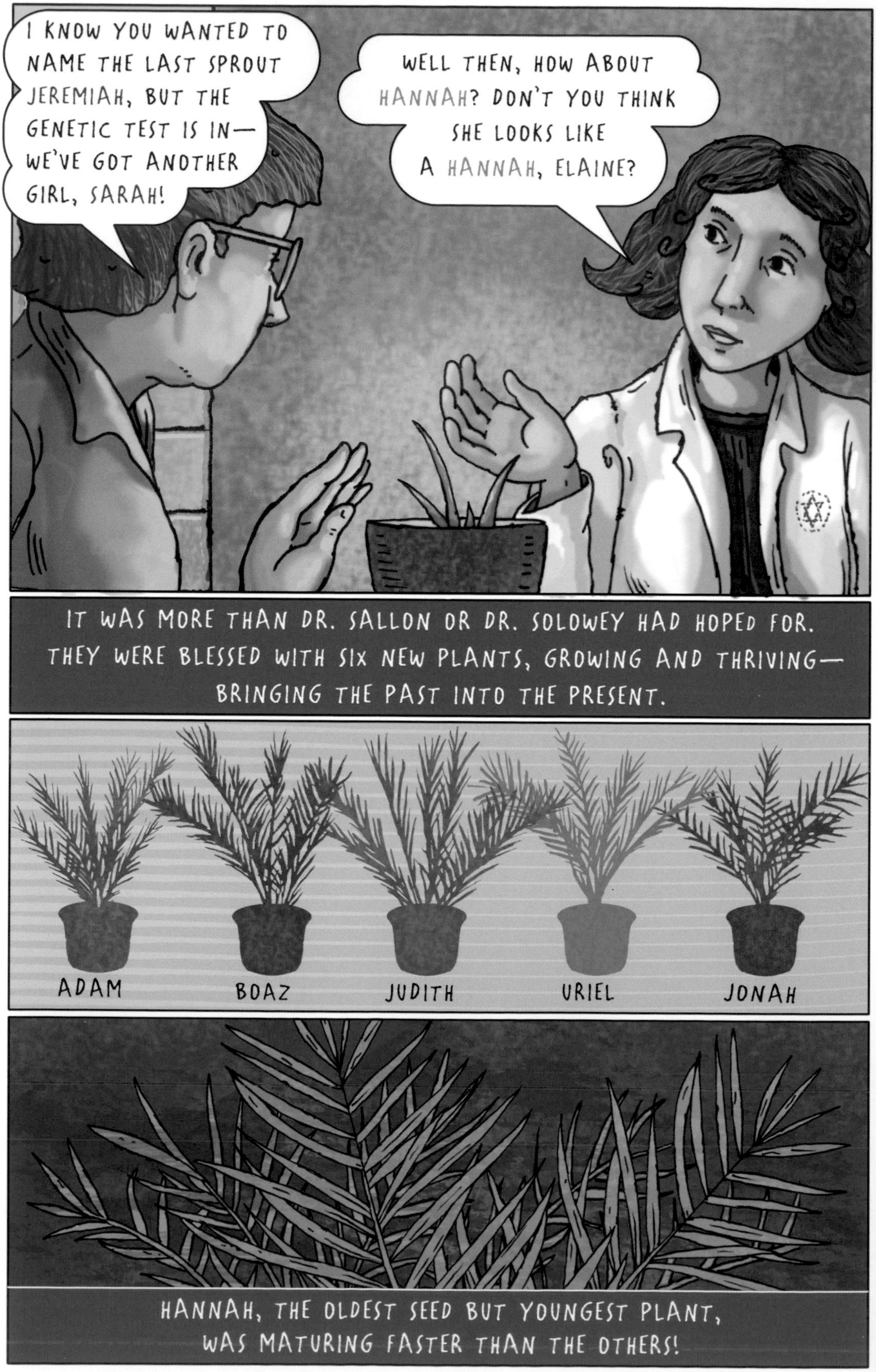
I KNOW YOU WANTED TO NAME THE LAST SPROUT JEREMIAH, BUT THE GENETIC TEST IS IN— WE'VE GOT ANOTHER GIRL, SARAH!
WELL THEN, HOW ABOUT HANNAH? DON'T YOU THINK SHE LOOKS LIKE A HANNAH, ELAINE?
IT WAS MORE THAN DR. SALLON OR DR. SOLOWEY HAD HOPED FOR. THEY WERE BLESSED WITH SIX NEW PLANTS, GROWING AND THRIVING— BRINGING THE PAST INTO THE PRESENT.
ADAM
BOAZ
JUDITH
URIEL
JONAH
HANNAH, THE OLDEST SEED BUT YOUNGEST PLANT, WAS MATURING FASTER THAN THE OTHERS!

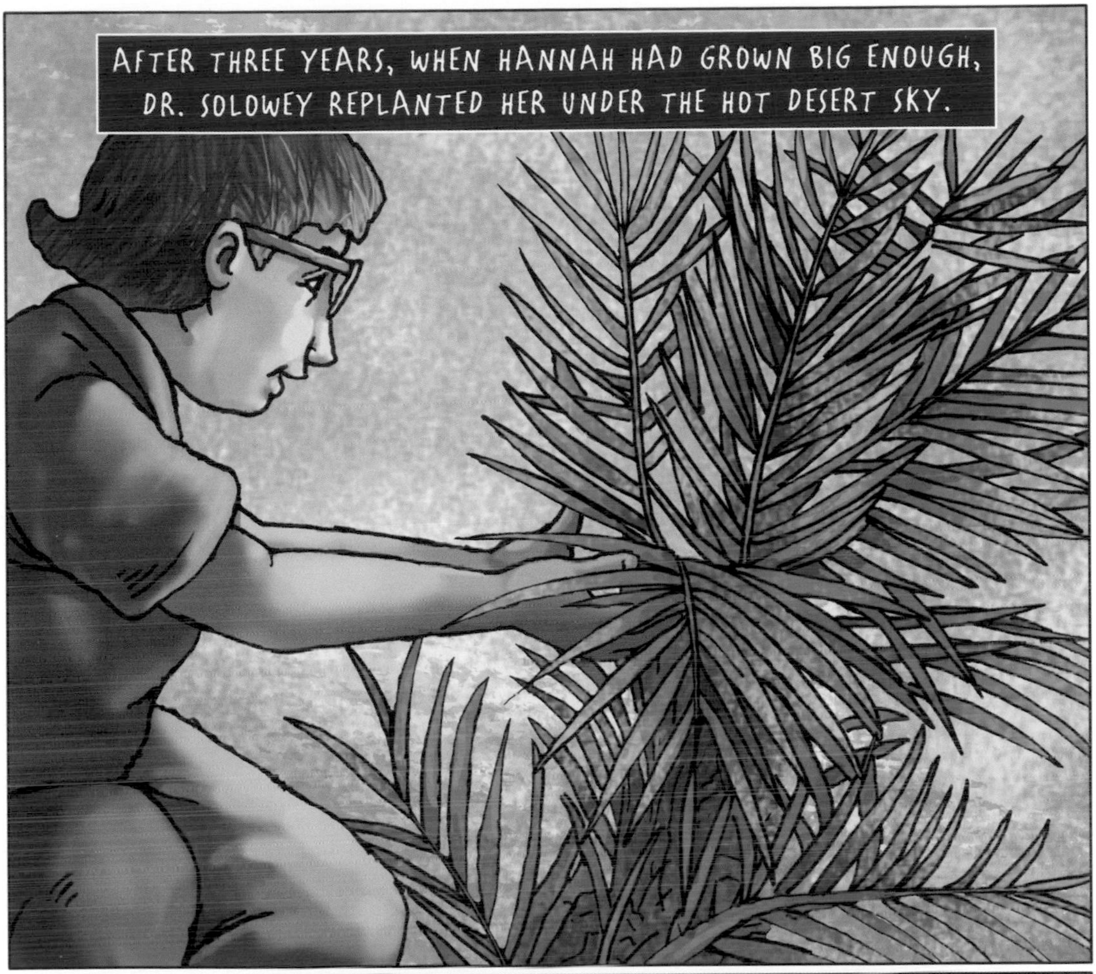
AFTER THREE YEARS, WHEN HANNAH HAD GROWN BIG ENOUGH, DR. SOLOWEY REPLANTED HER UNDER THE HOT DESERT SKY.

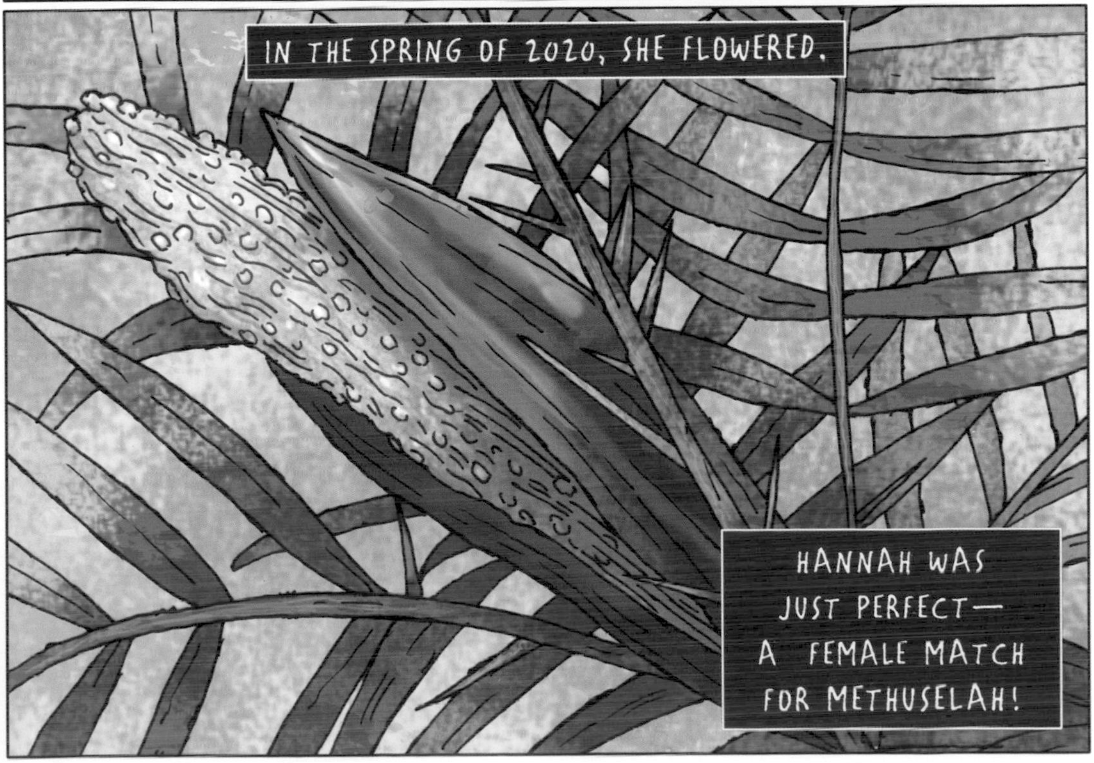
IN THE SPRING OF 2020, SHE FLOWERED.
HANNAH WAS JUST PERFECT— A FEMALE MATCH FOR METHUSELAH!

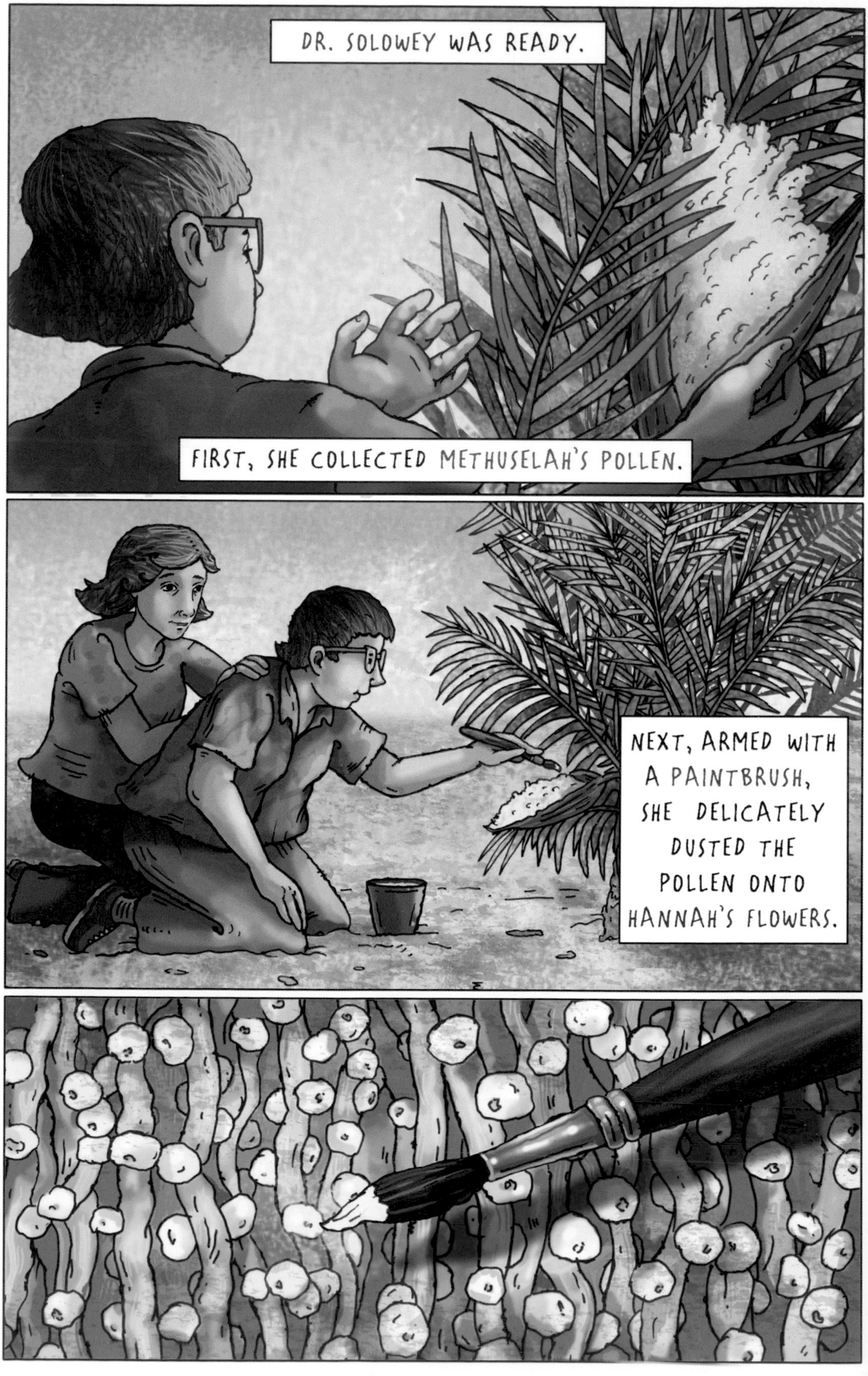
DR. SOLOWEY WAS READY.
FIRST, SHE COLLECTED METHUSELAH'S POLLEN.
NEXT, ARMED WITH A PAINTBRUSH, SHE DELICATELY DUSTED THE POLLEN ONTO HANNAH'S FLOWERS.

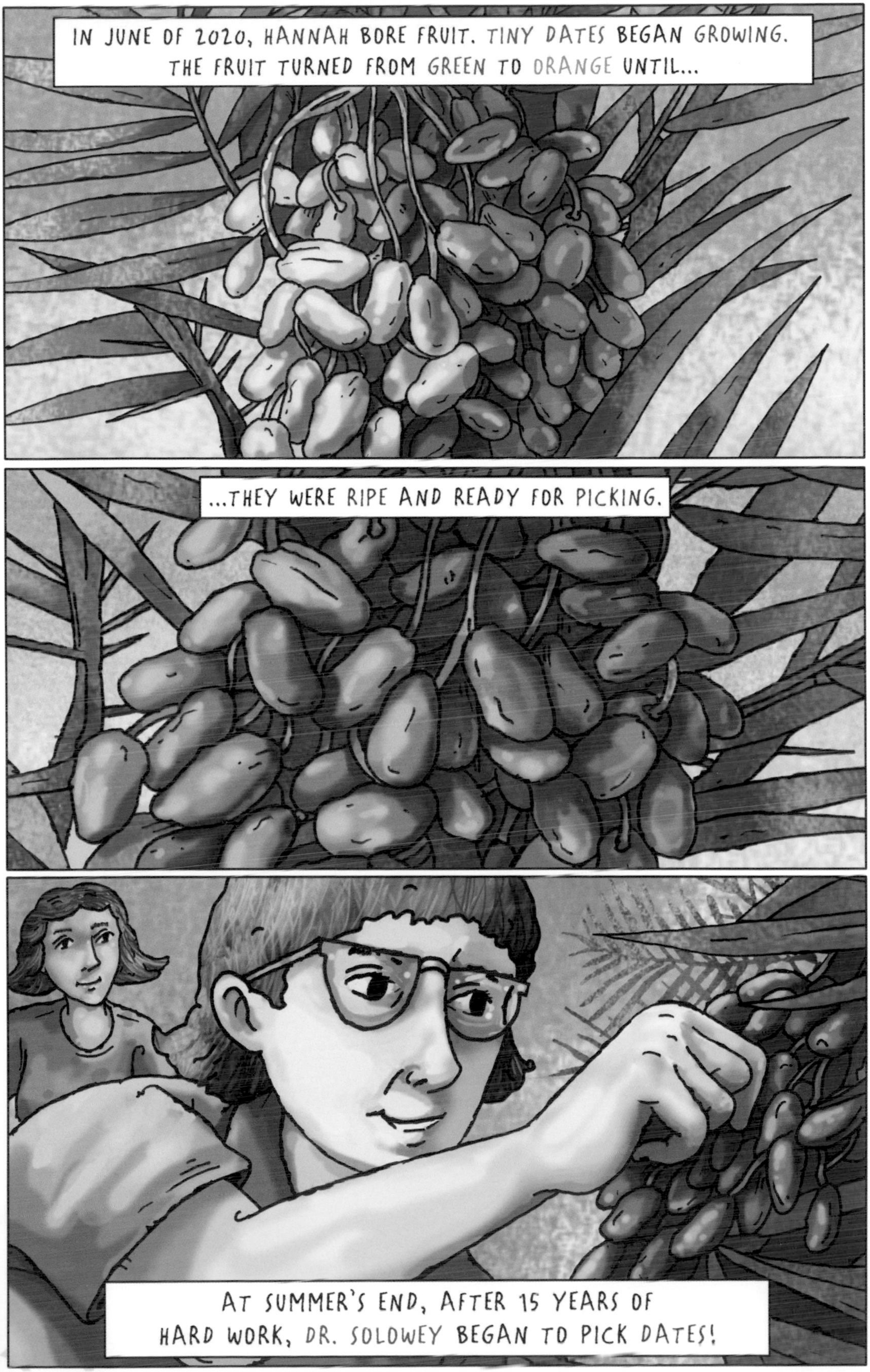
IN JUNE OF 2020, HANNAH BORE FRUIT. TINY DATES BEGAN GROWING. THE FRUIT TURNED FROM GREEN TO ORANGE UNTIL...
...THEY WERE RIPE AND READY FOR PICKING.
AT SUMMER'S END, AFTER 15 YEARS OF HARD WORK, DR. SOLOWEY BEGAN TO PICK DATES!

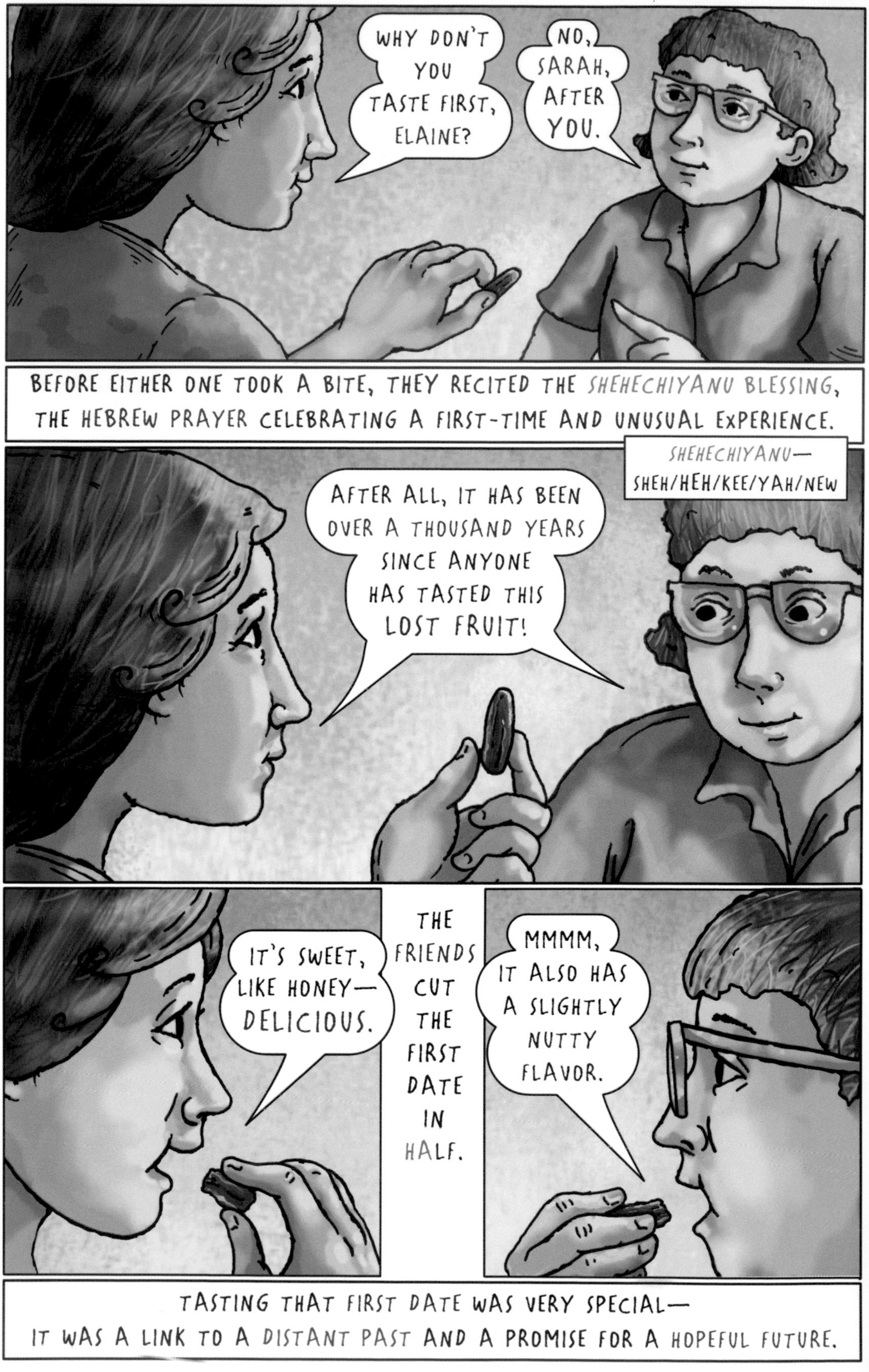
WHY DON'T YOU TASTE FIRST, ELAINE?
NO, SARAH, AFTER YOU.
BEFORE EITHER ONE TOOK A BITE, THEY RECITED THE SHEHECHIYANU BLESSING, THE HEBREW PRAYER CELEBRATING A FIRST-TIME AND UNUSUAL EXPERIENCE.
SHEHECHIYANU— SHEH/HEH/KEE/YAH/NEW
AFTER ALL, IT HAS BEEN OVER A THOUSAND YEARS SINCE ANYONE HAS TASTED THIS LOST FRUIT!
IT'S SWEET, LIKE HONEY— DELICIOUS.
THE FRIENDS CUT THE FIRST DATE IN HALF.
MMMM, IT ALSO HAS A SLIGHTLY NUTTY FLAVOR.
TASTING THAT FIRST DATE WAS VERY SPECIAL— IT WAS A LINK TO A DISTANT PAST AND A PROMISE FOR A HOPEFUL FUTURE.

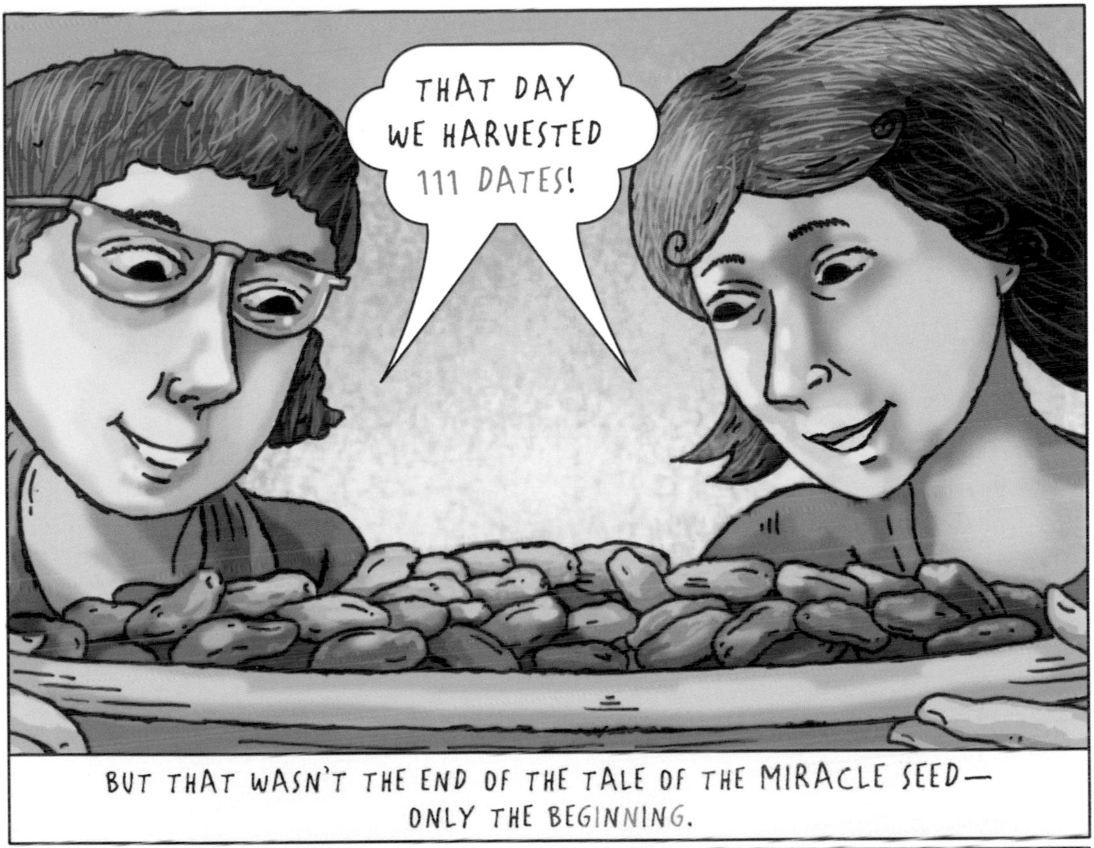
THAT DAY WE HARVESTED 111 DATES!
BUT THAT WASN'T THE END OF THE TALE OF THE MIRACLE SEED— ONLY THE BEGINNING.

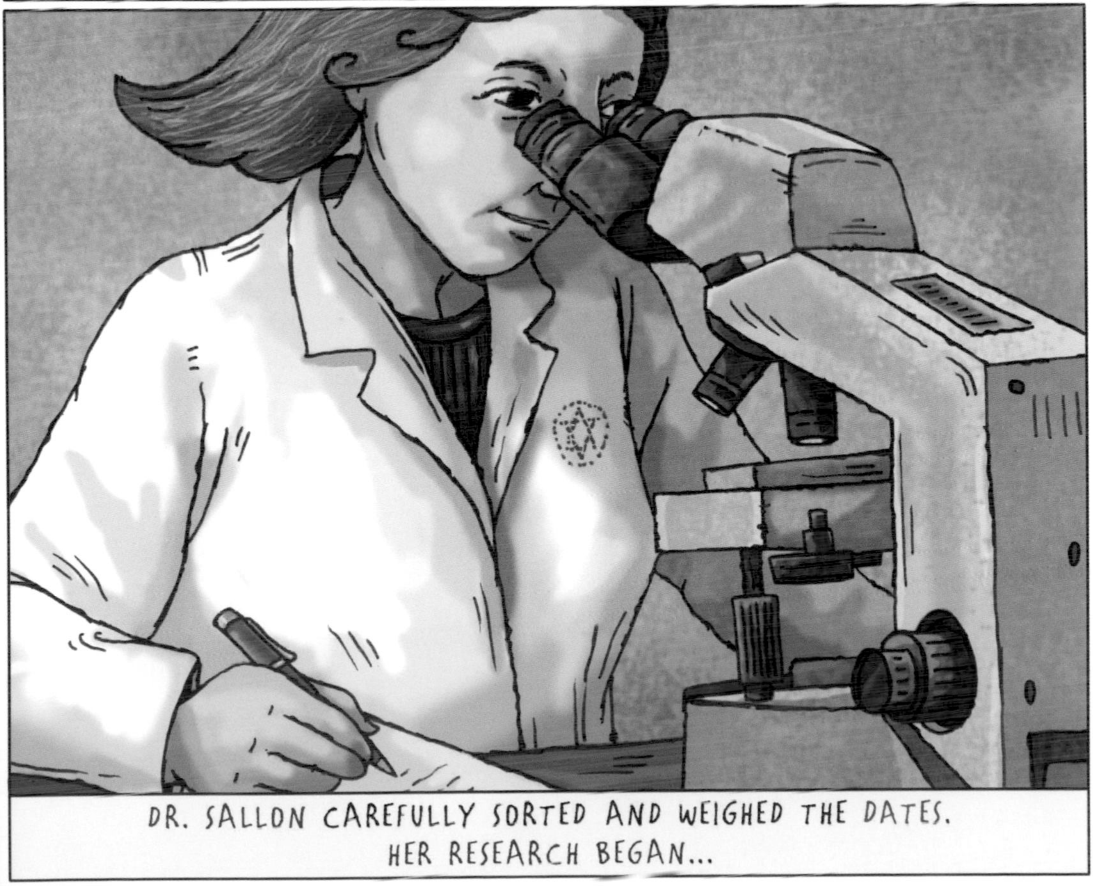
DR. SALLON CAREFULLY SORTED AND WEIGHED THE DATES. HER RESEARCH BEGAN...

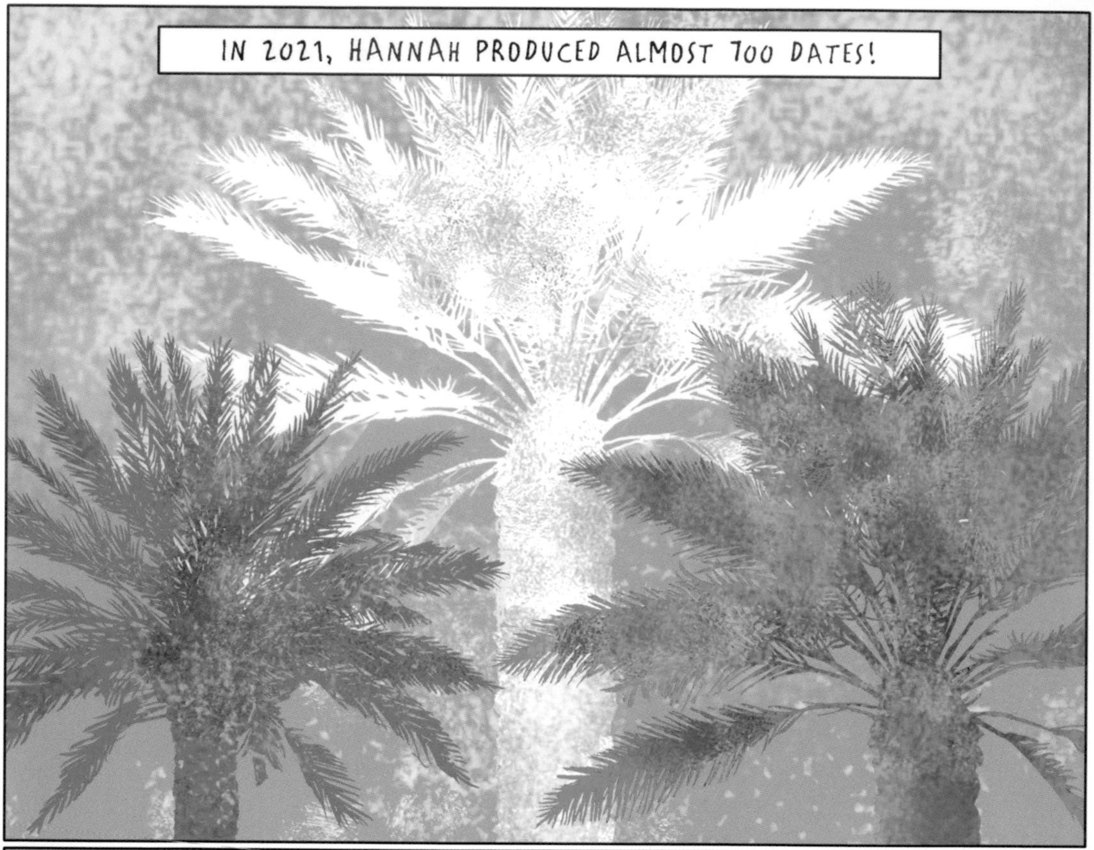
IN 2021, HANNAH PRODUCED ALMOST 700 DATES!

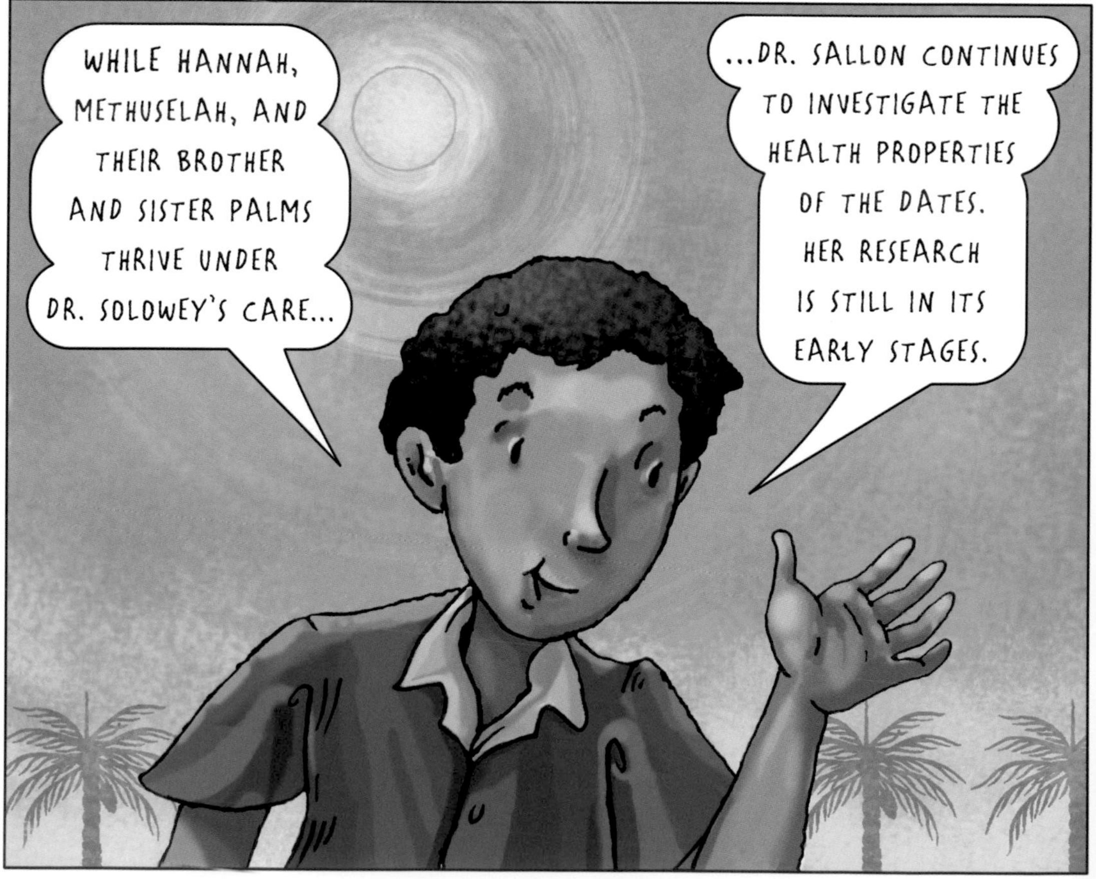
WHILE HANNAH, METHUSELAH, AND THEIR BROTHER AND SISTER PALMS THRIVE UNDER DR. SOLOWEY'S CARE...
...DR. SALLON CONTINUES TO INVESTIGATE THE HEALTH PROPERTIES OF THE DATES. HER RESEARCH IS STILL IN ITS EARLY STAGES.

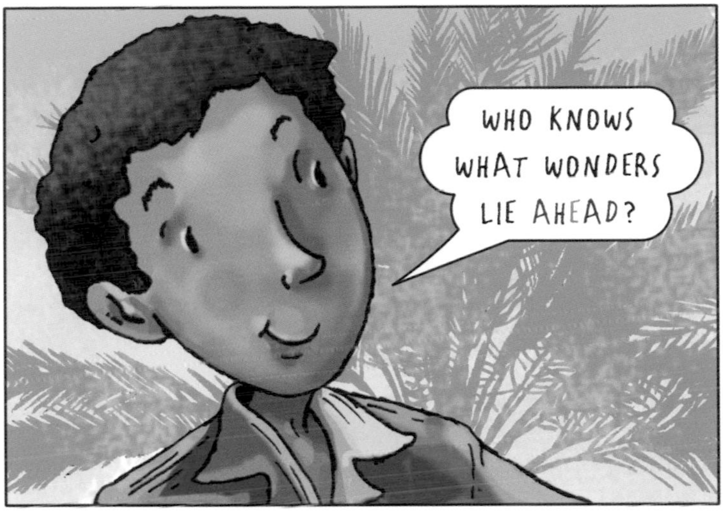
WHO KNOWS WHAT WONDERS LIE AHEAD?

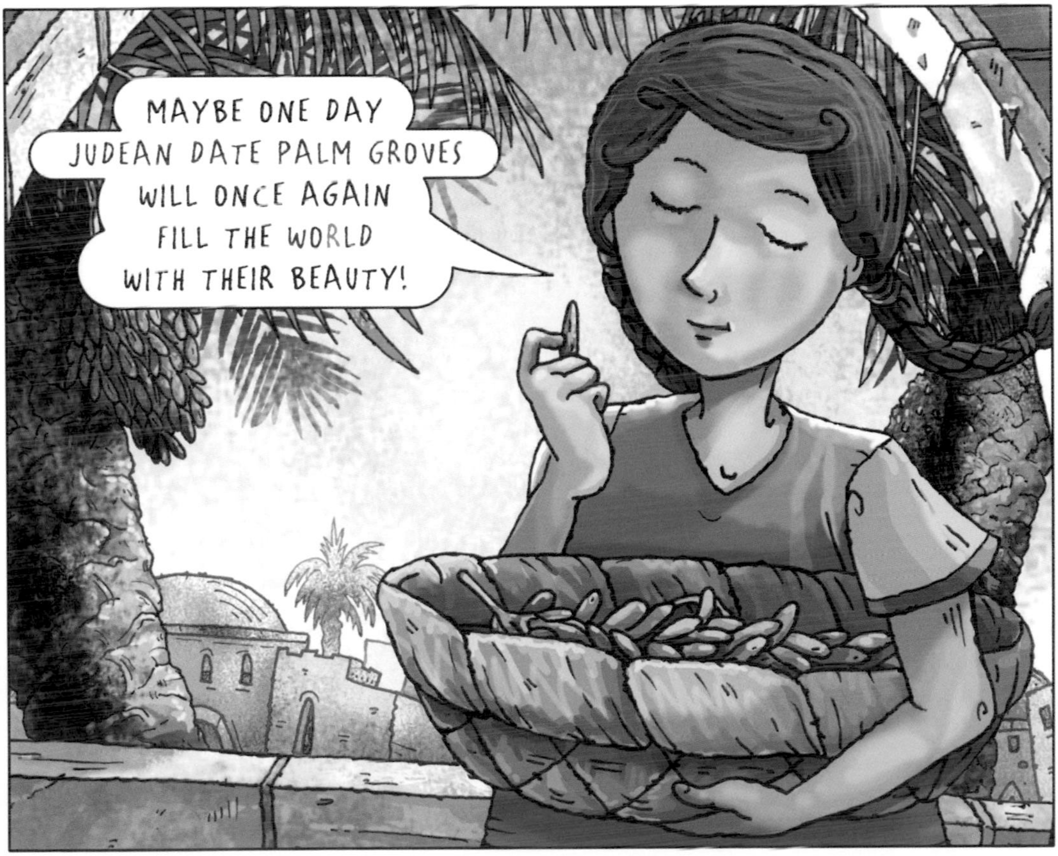
MAYBE ONE DAY JUDEAN DATE PALM GROVES WILL ONCE AGAIN FILL THE WORLD WITH THEIR BEAUTY!

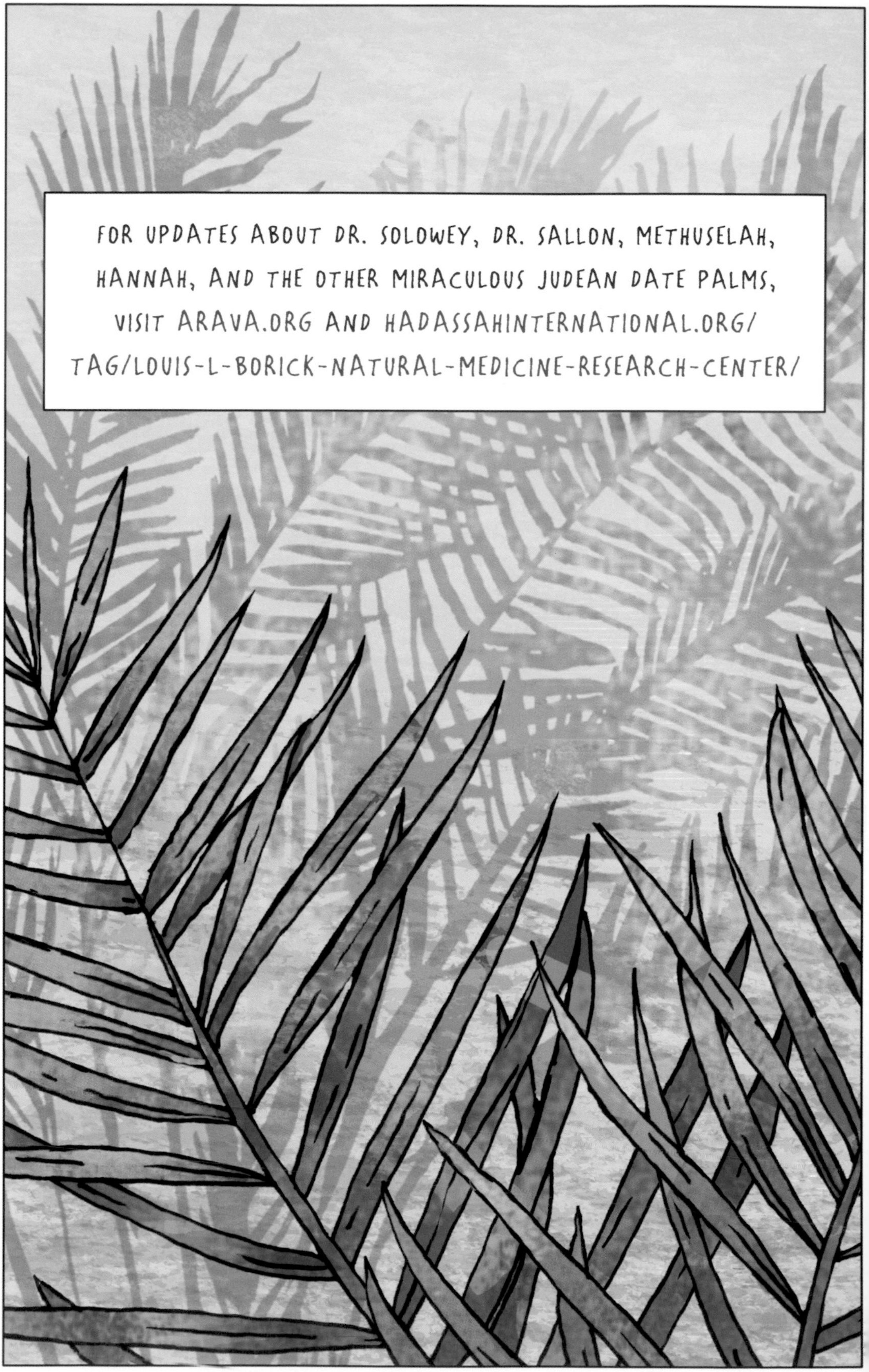
FOR UPDATES ABOUT DR. SOLOWEY, DR. SALLON, METHUSELAH, HANNAH, AND THE OTHER MIRACULOUS JUDEAN DATE PALMS, VISIT ARAVA.ORG AND HADASSAHINTERNATIONAL.ORG/TAG/LOUIS-L-BORICK-NATURAL-MEDICINE-RESEARCH-CENTER/

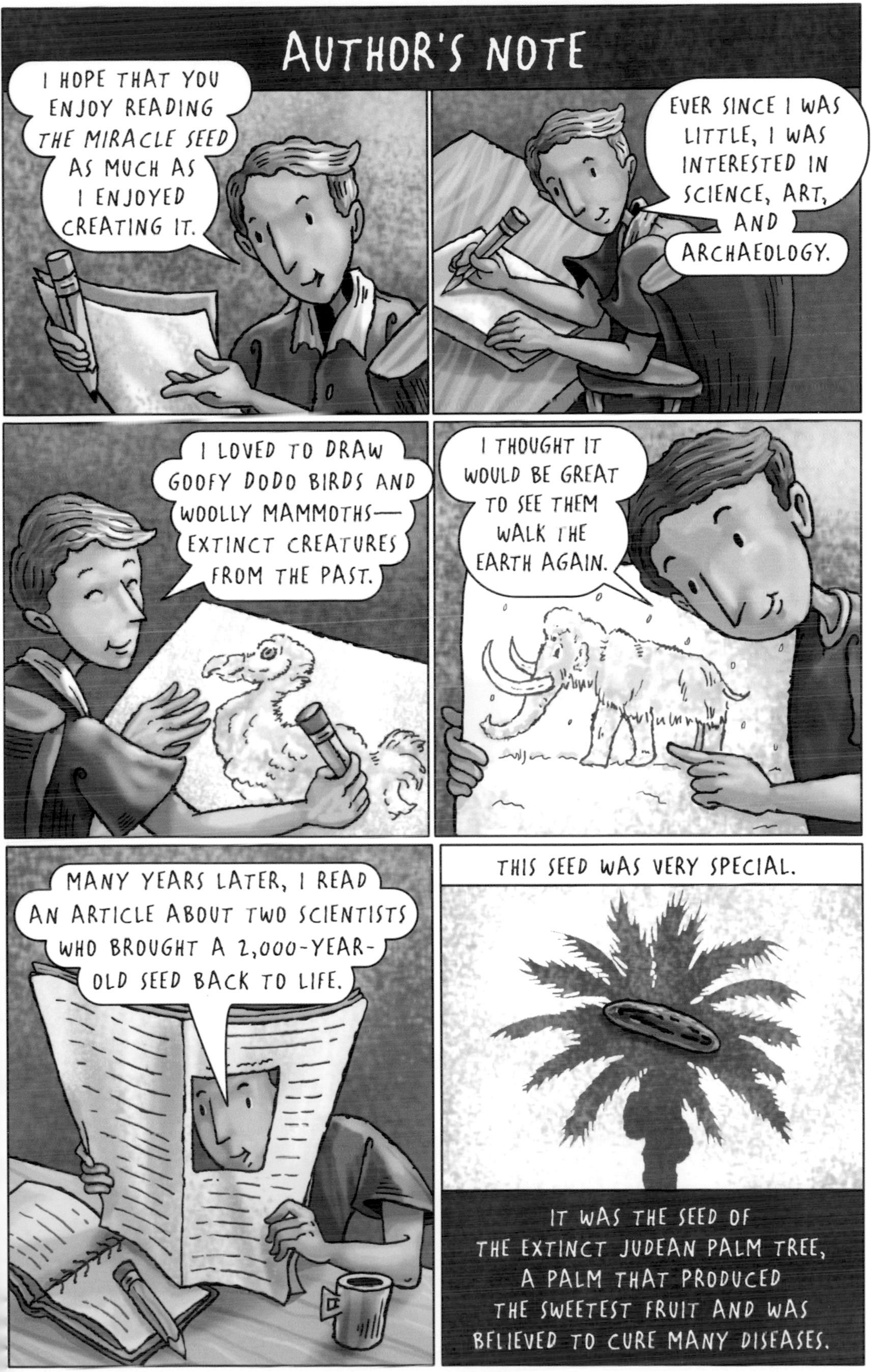
AUTHOR'S NOTE
I HOPE THAT YOU ENJOY READING THE MIRACLE SEED AS MUCH AS I ENJOYED CREATING IT.
EVER SINCE I WAS LITTLE, I WAS INTERESTED IN SCIENCE, ART, AND ARCHAEOLOGY.
I LOVED TO DRAW GOOFY DODO BIRDS AND WOOLLY MAMMOTHS— EXTINCT CREATURES FROM THE PAST.
I THOUGHT IT WOULD BE GREAT TO SEE THEM WALK THE EARTH AGAIN.
MANY YEARS LATER, I READ AN ARTICLE ABOUT TWO SCIENTISTS WHO BROUGHT A 2,000-YEAR-OLD SEED BACK TO LIFE.
THIS SEED WAS VERY SPECIAL.
IT WAS THE SEED OF THE EXTINCT JUDEAN PALM TREE, A PALM THAT PRODUCED THE SWEETEST FRUIT AND WAS BELIEVED TO CURE MANY DISEASES.

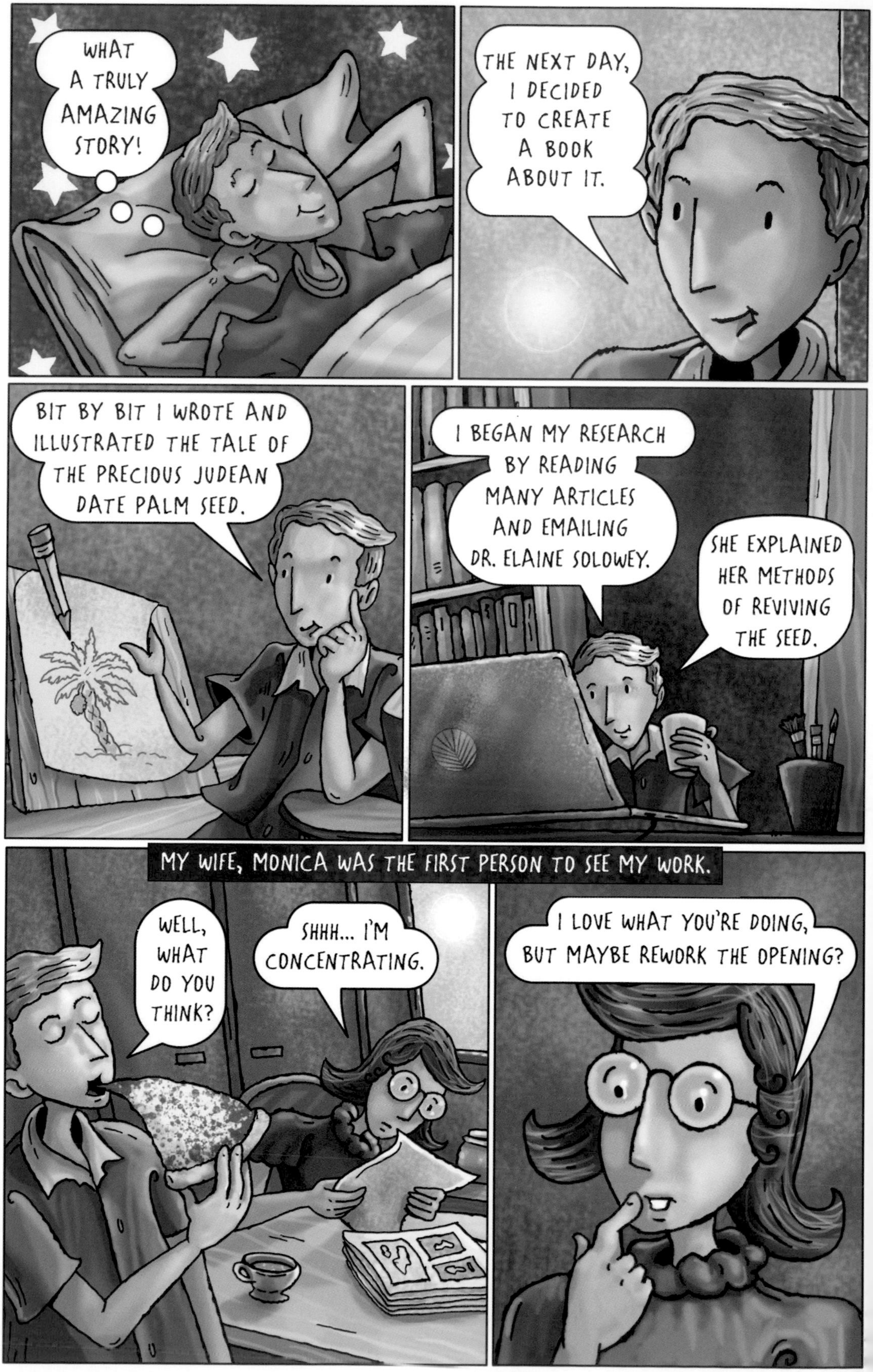
WHAT A TRULY AMAZING STORY!
THE NEXT DAY, I DECIDED TO CREATE A BOOK ABOUT IT.
BIT BY BIT I WROTE AND ILLUSTRATED THE TALE OF THE PRECIOUS JUDEAN DATE PALM SEED.
I BEGAN MY RESEARCH BY READING MANY ARTICLES AND EMAILING DR. ELAINE SOLOWEY.
SHE EXPLAINED HER METHODS OF REVIVING THE SEED.
MY WIFE, MONICA WAS THE FIRST PERSON TO SEE MY WORK.
WELL, WHAT DO YOU THINK?
SHHH... I'M CONCENTRATING.
I LOVE WHAT YOU'RE DOING, BUT MAYBE REWORK THE OPENING?

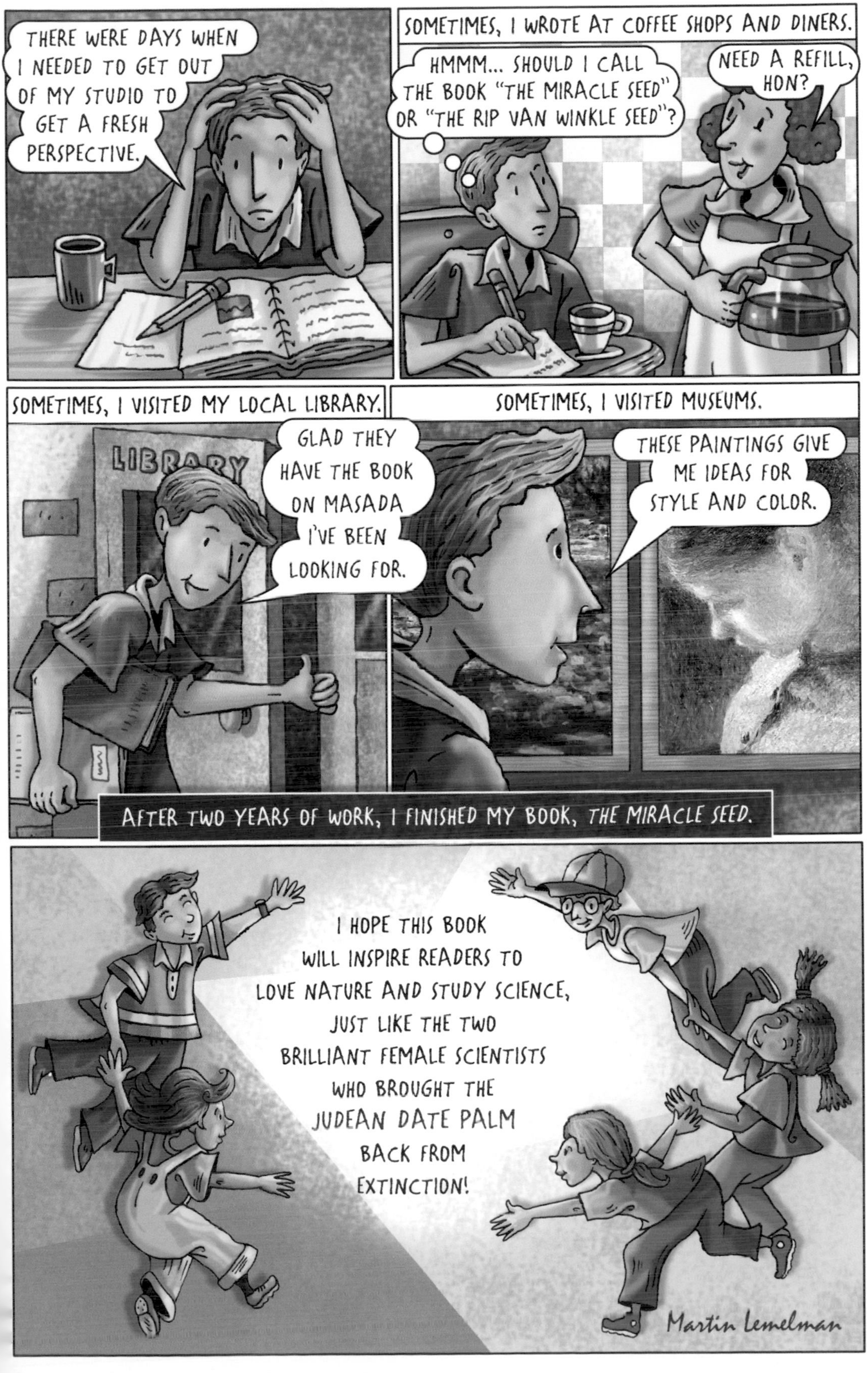
THERE WERE DAYS WHEN I NEEDED TO GET OUT OF MY STUDIO TO GET A FRESH PERSPECTIVE.
SOMETIMES, I WROTE AT COFFEE SHOPS AND DINERS.
HMMM... SHOULD I CALL THE BOOK "THE MIRACLE SEED" OR "THE RIP VAN WINKLE SEED"?
NEED A REFILL, HON?
SOMETIMES, I VISITED MY LOCAL LIBRARY.
LIBRARY
GLAD THEY HAVE THE BOOK ON MASADA I'VE BEEN LOOKING FOR.
SOMETIMES, I VISITED MUSEUMS.
THESE PAINTINGS GIVE ME IDEAS FOR STYLE AND COLOR.
AFTER TWO YEARS OF WORK, I FINISHED MY BOOK, *THE MIRACLE SEED.*
I HOPE THIS BOOK WILL INSPIRE READERS TO LOVE NATURE AND STUDY SCIENCE, JUST LIKE THE TWO BRILLIANT FEMALE SCIENTISTS WHO BROUGHT THE JUDEAN DATE PALM BACK FROM EXTINCTION!
Martin Lemelman

TIME LINE OF EVENTS

c. 957 BCE — The First Temple is built by King Solomon in Jerusalem. During this time, the Judean date palm becomes known as a symbol of the kingdom of Judah.

c. 587 BCE — The First Temple is destroyed by King Nebuchadnezzar of Babylon.

63 BCE — The Roman general Pompey captures Jerusalem, beginning Rome's rule over Judea and Israel.

20–10 BCE — King Herod renovates and enlarges the Second Temple in Jerusalem.

66–70 CE — The First Jewish Revolt, in which the Jewish people rebel against tyrannical Roman rule. In 70 CE, Jerusalem falls, the Second Temple is destroyed, and the Jewish state collapses.

73–74 CE — The Siege of Masada, in which the last Jewish stronghold falls to the Romans.

500–1400 CE? — Extinction of the Judean date palm. Whether through climate change or war, the Judean date palm vanishes approximately a thousand years ago.

1095–1291 CE — Western European Christians launch a series of crusades (religious wars) attempting to remove the Islamic rulers of the Holy Land. The violence and destruction of this period may have contributed to the Judean date palm's decline.

c. 1700s CE — No traces of the Judean date palm groves remain.

1948 CE — The Israeli Declaration of Independence establishes the State of Israel.

1963–1965 CE — Yigael Yadin and his team excavate Masada. They uncover many artifacts, including a jar containing 2,000-year-old Judean date palm seeds—including the future Adam and Methuselah.

1963–1991 CE	More ancient date seeds—including the future Judith, Boaz, Jonah, Uriel, and Hannah—are uncovered by archaeological excavations and surveys at Qumran, Wadi Makukh (a winter water channel in the Judean Desert), and Wadi Qelt (a valley, river gulch, or stream that runs from Jerusalem to Jericho).
2004 CE	Dr. Sarah Sallon receives permission from the Israel Antiquities Authority to see if three of the 2,000-year-old Judean date palm seeds can be revived.
January 25, 2005 CE	On Tu B'Shvat, the Jewish New Year of Trees, Dr. Elaine Solowey plants the ancient seeds. Six weeks later, one sprouts and is named Methuselah.
2011 CE	Methuselah flowers and is found to be a male date palm.
2011 CE	Dr. Sallon, hoping to find a female match for Methuselah, searches for and finds more ancient Judean date palm seeds.
2011 CE	Dr. Solowey plants the seeds. Two are female. Dr. Sallon and Dr. Solowey name them Judith and Hannah.
2019 CE	Adam, Jonah, and Hannah are transplanted from their greenhouse to the Arava Institute's Daniel Fischel & Sylvia Neil Research & Visitors' Park in the Negev Desert.
Spring 2020 CE	Hannah flowers for the first time. Dr. Solowey pollinates her with the pollen from Methuselah.
June 2020 CE	Hannah bears fruit for the first time.
End of Summer 2020 CE	One hundred and eleven Judean date palm dates are harvested from Hannah. The Judean date palm is officially no longer extinct!
Today	Hannah continues to thrive and produce fruit, and research continues on the Judean date palm and how it might be used to treat diseases.

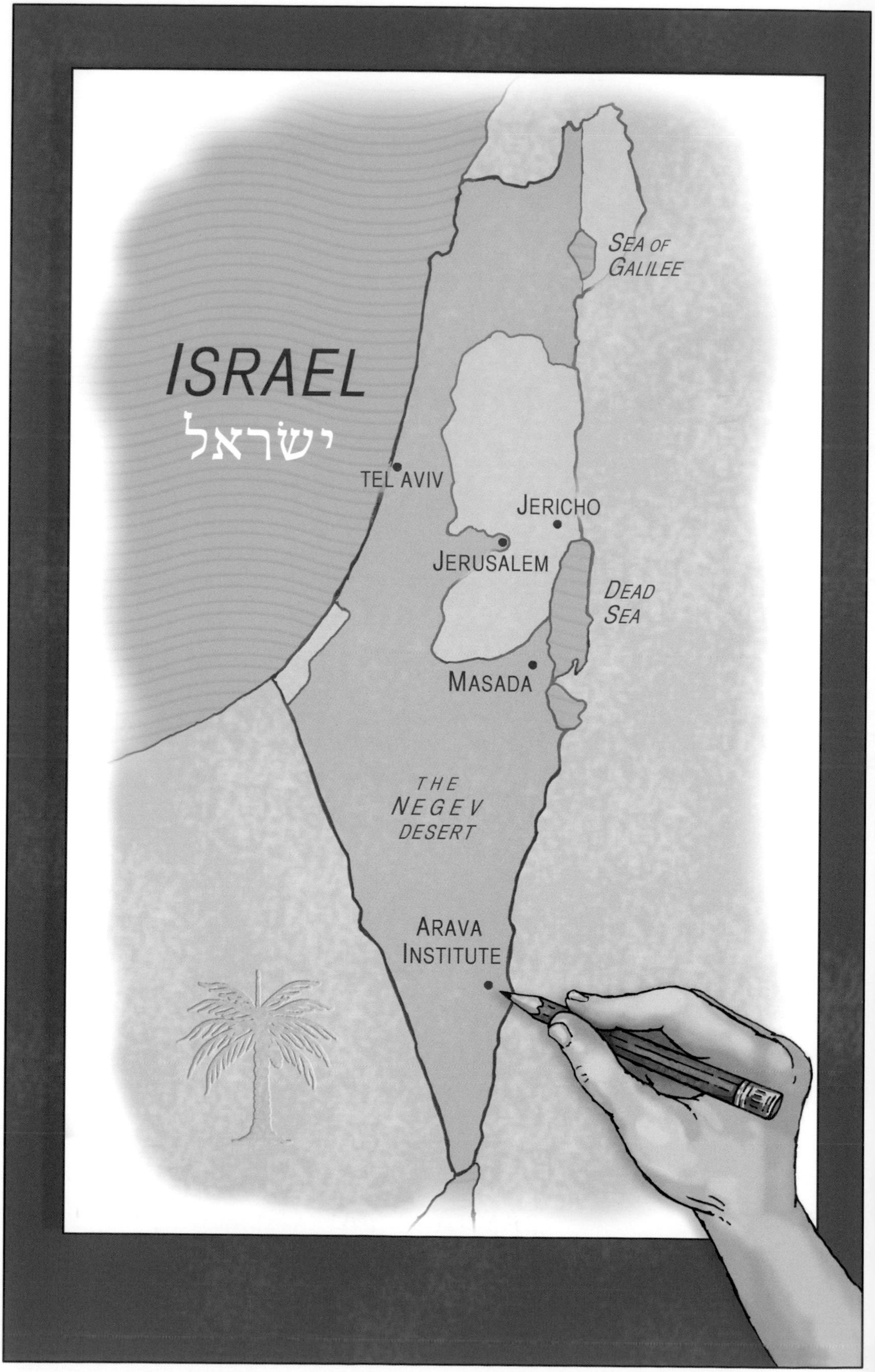
ISRAEL
ישראל
SEA OF GALILEE
TEL AVIV
JERICHO
JERUSALEM
DEAD SEA
MASADA
THE NEGEV DESERT
ARAVA INSTITUTE

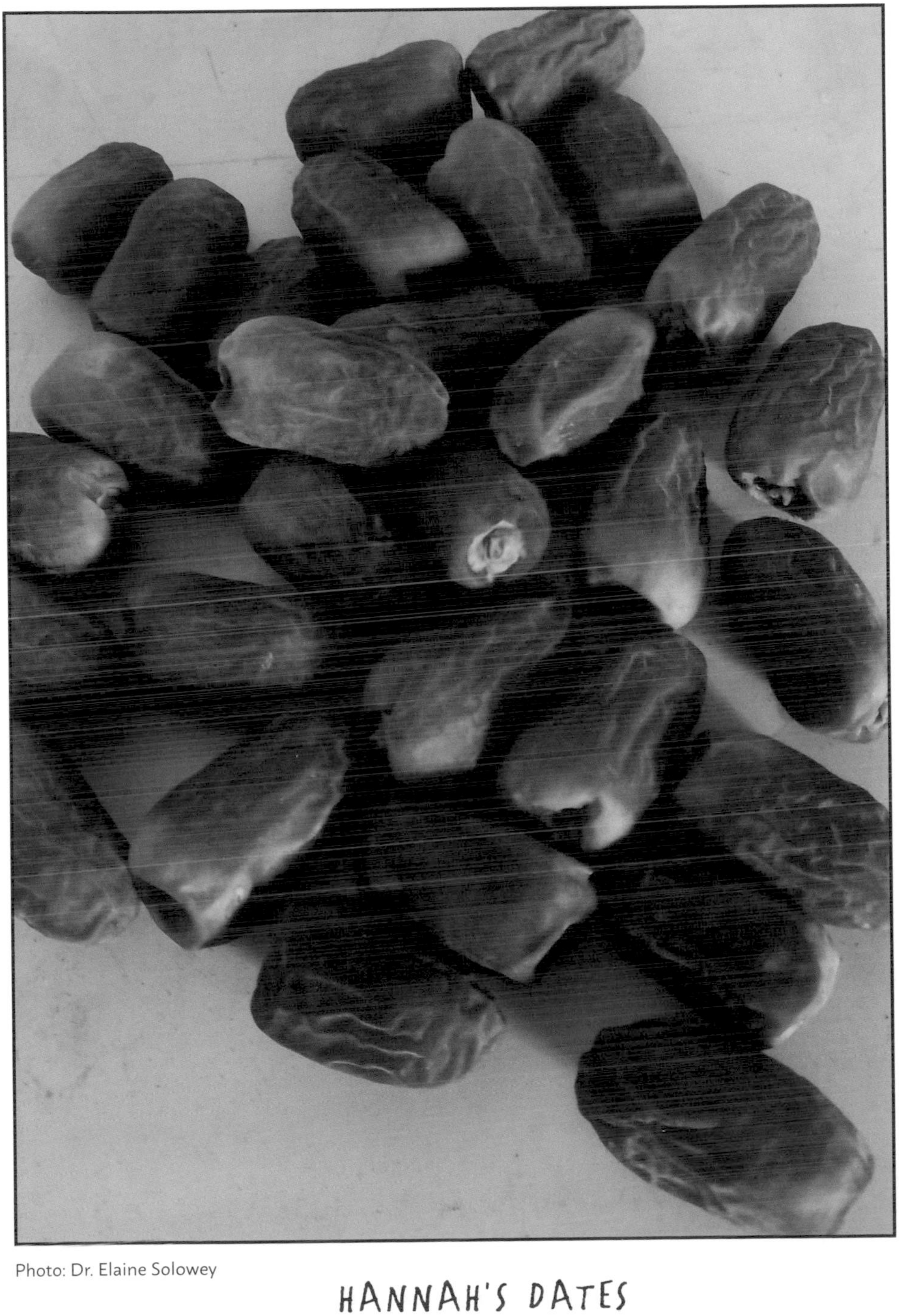

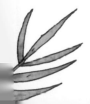

Photo: Dr. Elaine Solowey

HANNAH'S DATES

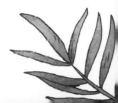

Photo: Dr. Elaine Solowey

METHUSELAH

Photo: Dr. Elaine Solowey

HANNAH